TWO PATCH
SCRAP QUILTS

PAT YAMIN

American Quilter's Society
P. O. Box 3290 • Paducah, KY 42002-3290
www.AmericanQuilter.com

Located in Paducah, Kentucky, the American Quilter's Society (AQS) is dedicated to promoting the accomplishments of today's quilters. Through its publications and events, AQS strives to honor today's quiltmakers and their work and to inspire future creativity and innovation in quiltmaking.

EXECUTIVE BOOK EDITOR: ANDI MILAM REYNOLDS
COPY EDITOR: BARBARA PITMAN
GRAPHIC DESIGN: ELAINE WILSON
ILLUSTRATIONS: LYNDA SMITH
COVER DESIGN: MICHAEL BUCKINGHAM
PHOTOGRAPHY: CHARLES R. LYNCH

Additional copies of this book may be ordered from the American Quilter's Society, PO Box 3290, Paducah, KY 42002-3290, or online at www.AmericanQuilter.com.

Text © 2011, Author, Pat Yamin
Artwork © 2011, American Quilter's Society

LIBRARY OF CONGRESS CATALOGING-IN-PUBLICATION DATA
Yamin, Pat.
  Two patch scrap quilts / by Pat Yamin.
    p. cm.
  Summary: "Directions and templates for hand or machine piecing are given for 21 classic Two-Patch patterns in three quilt sizes-63 possible projects"--Provided by publisher.
  ISBN 978-1-60460-002-5
  1. Patchwork--Patterns. 2. Quilting--Patterns. I. Title. II. Title: 2 patch scrap quilts.
  TT835.Y377 2011
  746.46'041--dc23
                                2011032631

COVER: SPINNING SPOOLS, detail. Full quilt on page 103.
TITLE PAGE: JOSEPH'S COAT, detail. Full quilt on page 49.
ABOVE AND OPPOSITE: DRUNKARD'S PATH, detail. Full quilt on page 27.

CONTENTS

LEFT AND OPPOSITE: SNOWBALL, detail. Full quilt on page 99.

BASIC DIRECTIONS

The beauty of working with just two patches to create quilt blocks is simplicity. Blocks made of two patches provide a highly satisfying piecing experience, whether by hand or machine.

SEWING SUPPLIES

Template plastic
Sharpie® fine point pen
Rulers
    6" x 12"
    6" x 24"
    6½" x 6½"
Craft scissors
Rotary cutter and mat
Paper punch
Pins
Needles
    Machine
    Quilting betweens
    John James long darners #7

Thread
    Sewing
    Quilting
Mechanical pencil
Iron and ironing surface
Stiletto
Heat resistant plastic
Safety pins
Flannel folding wall
Masking tape

QUILT SIZE & NUMBER OF BLOCKS FOR SCRAP QUILTS

All of the patterns in the book are made with repeat blocks. **The total number to cut and sew is given for the sample quilt in the photograph.** If you want to make your quilt larger or smaller, adjust the number of blocks you make. Another way to enlarge a quilt is to add sashing and/or one or more borders.

Remember: Yardage estimates for these quilts are just that—estimates. You will be working with scraps—improvise!

SELECTING FABRIC

I used 42" wide fabric for my calculations and rounded it up to determine the yardage for sashing, borders, and binding. If you worry about shrinkage, add a quarter of a yard of fabric to my calculations as an added measure of protection. **The patterns for the quilt tops are based on the scrap idea, however, so you don't really need to know yardage for the blocks/tops.**

You can use your own fabric stash or exchange scrap pieces with friends, guild members, or neighbors. Buy fabric at quilt shops, quilt shows, or garage sales, or raid your grandmother's sewing room.

PREPARING THE FABRIC

Always prewash, dry, and press the fabric before you start. When I have small pieces, I put them in a lingerie bag so they don't become tangled in the washing machine. You can buy these bags at your local drugstore or supermarket in the laundry aisle. Or, if I only have a few pieces, I hand wash them in the sink and lay them out on a towel to dry.

If you are in the habit of washing your fabric when you bring it home from the store, you won't have to think about washing your scraps. To remember that you have washed a fabric, cut a small square off from one corner before you toss it into your scrap basket. Scrap quilts are really a history of our quilting and sewing projects.

MAKING TEMPLATES

Remember: The templates in this book include the seam allowance.

Use either plain or ¼" gridded plastic. Most of the patterns have straight edges, so I prefer gridded plastic (see Resources).

Tips:

○ Change your cutting blade and sewing machine needle after each project.

○ Always buy more fabric than you think you're going to use; you'll never be sorry.

○ Add a little "sizzle" to your quilt by using a color you normally would not choose.

○ After you wash and iron the fabric, before cutting, use spray starch to give the fabric extra body.

○ Hang large pieces of prepared fabric such as backings on pant hangers to keep them straight. No need to iron again!

Tips:

- It's a good idea to use just one brand of ruler on the same project. I like Omnigrid® rulers because the lines are so easy to read.

- Never share a previous cut; move the template 1/8" down the fabric strip, allowing each cut to be new.

- Cut the largest or longest pieces such as sashings and borders first.

- It's always a good idea to make one test block first. Are you happy with the colors, and is the block the accurate size?

For Machine Piecing

Lay the template plastic over the pattern in the book and trace around it with a fine point permanent marker. Cut out the template with craft scissors exactly on this cutting line.

The 1/4" seam allowance is included in the templates in this book. You can ignore the corner dots that are marked on the templates; these are for hand piecing.

For Hand Piecing

Lay the template plastic over the pattern in the book and trace around it with a fine point permanent marker. This is the cutting line. Measure in 1/4" and mark the stitching line. Mark the stitching corners with dots. Cut out the template with craft scissors exactly on the cutting line.

Use a paper punch to cut out the corner dots. Place the template on the wrong side of your fabric, trace around it and mark the corner dots. Draw the sewing lines from dot to dot on your fabric.

CUTTING

Measure the height of the template and use a ruler to cut your fabric into strips 1/2" taller than the template height. This will give you 1/4" on the top and bottom of the template to ensure accuracy when cutting strips. You can stack your fabric in two or four layers.

When cutting your fabric, pay attention to the pattern pieces that have reversed shapes. If you double-fold your fabric, you will automatically get a left and right pattern piece.

PIECING
By Machine

Check that you can achieve a 1/4" seam allowance on your sewing machine. If your machine does not have a 1/4" foot, then lift the presser foot and measure over exactly 1/4" from the needle. Lay a strip of masking tape at that point to help guide your fabric through the machine, keeping the 1/4" seam.

A good straight stitch is all you need for piecing. I prefer the stitch length to be 10 to 12 per inch. Place 2 pieces of fabric right sides together with raw edges aligned. There is no need to pin pieces shorter than 4". Begin and end stitching from the raw edges without backstitching.

Always finger press the units or blocks. If you must press with an iron, do so lightly so you don't stretch the fabric.

By Hand

Place 2 shapes together with right sides facing and place a pin through both of the pieces at the ¼" mark at either end. Stitch with a single thread no longer than 18". To secure the stitch, begin at the ¼" seam line, take a stitch and then backstitch without making a knot.

Use a quilting betweens needle to sew the pieces with an even running stitch beside the drawn seam line as straight as possible. Backstitch at the end of the seam line. Press the seams toward the darker fabric.

DESIGN WALL

You can turn any wall in your sewing space into a design wall by attaching a large piece of flannel to it. Or try using a piece of foam core wrapped with flannel. Cut the foam core to the size you will need, pull the flannel taut over it, and bring the flannel to the back. Secure it with masking tape. Fabric that is finger pressed lightly onto the flannel will cling to it, allowing you to arrange and rearrange pieces in your blocks. Sometimes I leave the blocks up for a few days to see if I really like the result.

Make one test block first to audition the scraps.

PIECING THE QUILT

Pin pieces together before sewing. The piecing directions are given with each pattern.

Tips:

○ Have a "ready-to-go" bag packed with a hand sewing project. You can get a lot accomplished in several small minutes of time.

○ Use black flannel for a design wall background if you are using a lot of colors; it helps with the design process.

○ If you finger press your seams in opposite directions where they meet, your top will lie flatter.

Tips:

○ Sewing a mitered border from the quilt top corner to the outer edge of the border strip minimizes stretching and distortion.

○ Before basting, lightly press the top on the wrong side first, then the right side, to prevent seam allowance pleats. Cut off loose threads front and back and repair any open seams.

○ Cut backing and batting 2" to 4" wider/longer than the quilt top. If someone else will quilt your top, ask them about the dimensions they prefer for batting and backing.

○ Thread baste for hand quilting; pin baste for machine quilting.

MITERING A BORDER

Attach a border strip to the quilt side. To get the correct border strip length, measure the quilt side length plus the border width multiplied by 2 and add the seam allowance. For example, if the side is 10" long and the border is 4½" wide, cut the border 19½" long. Match and pin the quilt side center to the border strip center. Sew the border strip to the quilt side, starting and stopping ¼" from the quilt top edge. The border strip should extend beyond the quilt top on either end by 4½".

Attach the other three borders in this same manner. Then lay adjacent borders over each other right-sides together and pin. Draw a 45-degree line from the quilt top corner to the end of the border seam. Sew along that line from the quilt top corner to the outer edge of the border strip. Trim away excess seam allowance to ¼" and press the seam open.

Repeat this procedure for the remaining three corners.

QUILT THE QUILT

Buy the same quality fabric for the backing as you used for the top, maybe a floral or tone-on-tone. Or, go wild and piece the back from scraps. If you need to sew a long vertical or horizontal seam, sew it with a ½" seam for strength and press open.

Compare batts with how you plan to quilt the quilt so the experience is enjoyable and yields the results you desire.

Baste the three layers—backing spread wrong-side up, batting smoothed out several times, the ironed top laid right-side up. In a radiating pattern from the center out, either thread or safety pin baste. Check the batting label for how far apart basting lines should be.

Hand or machine quilt as desired. For specific tips on quilting, see my website, www.comequiltwithme.com.

BINDING

Either straight grain or bias binding will work. Binding yardage in this book is based on straight grain binding. You should measure your quilt to determine the exact yardage you need. Use your favorite binding method.

QUILT LABEL

There are many commercial labels made today to choose from. If you have an embroidery program with your machine, you can be very creative.

Being old-fashioned, on a 4" x 6" piece of fabric, I use a permanent ink pen in either black or brown. I include the name of the pattern, who made the quilt, the recipient's name, and the special occasion (if there was one). I also write the month, day, and year I finished the quilt. Then I stitch this label by hand to the back of the quilt.

On some of the project and gallery quilts in this book you will see two names; one is the block name, and the one in parentheses comes from the quiltmaker's label.

As a bonus, I sometimes stitch a few extra pieces of fabric to the back should a repair be needed at a future date. I got this idea from the person who restores my antique quilts. She uses a tiny brass pin to attach the old fabric piece to the back of the quilt for historical purposes.

MAKING A SLEEVE

If you'd like to hang your quilt to display it, cut a strip of your backing fabric or muslin that is 8½" wide and 2" shorter than the width of the finished quilt. If you can, use your backing fabric so it will blend in.

Turn under and stitch the two ends with a ¼" seam. Fold and press the strip in half lengthwise, right-sides together, and stitch the length. Turn the sleeve inside out and iron it flat. Position the top of the sleeve so that it touches the bottom edge of the binding on the back and stitch it to the quilt back by hand. Allow about ¼" of play so a rod can pass through the sleeve without distorting the quilt front. Hand stitch the bottom edge to the back of the quilt.

Don't stress over your two patch quilt. Have fun!

Two Patch Scrap Quilts

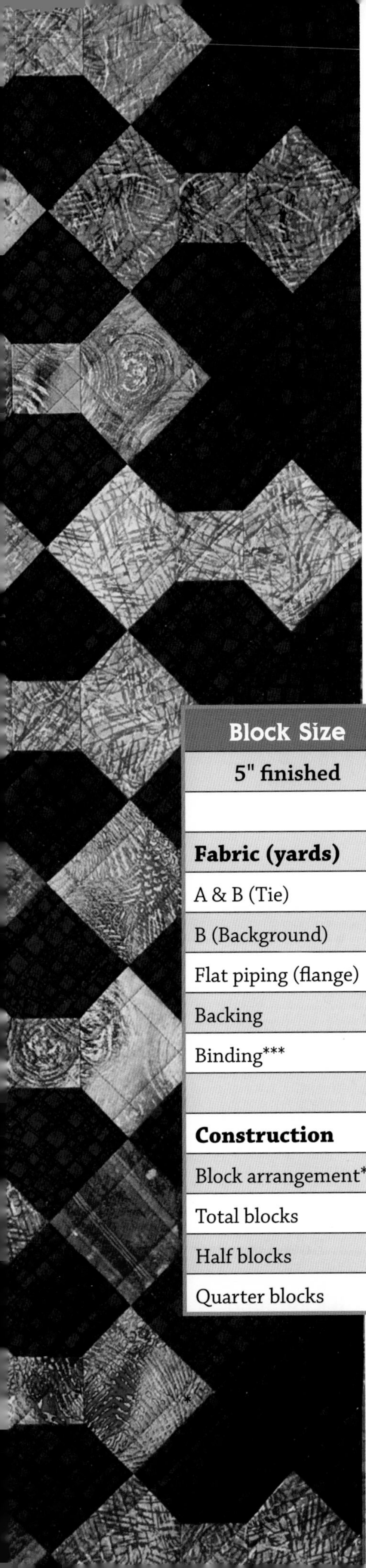

BOW TIE

Made by Margrette Carr
San Diego, California
(See page 17)

This can be a planned quilt with specific color choices or lots of scraps for variety. Margrette chose a rainbow look for the ties and a uniform background and then set the blocks on point.

Block Size	Sample Quilt*	Twin**	Queen**
5" finished	36¼" x 42½"	65" x 90"	85" x 95"
Fabric (yards)			
A & B (Tie)	1¾	4¼	6
B (Background)	2½	2½	4
Flat piping (flange)	¼ (9" x 36")	☆	☆
Backing	1¼	5	8¾
Binding***	½	½	¾
Construction			
Block arrangement*	5 x 6	13 x 18	17 x 19
Total blocks	50	234	323
Half blocks	18	☆	☆
Quarter blocks	4	☆	☆

   *   Blocks set on point.
  **   Blocks set straight.
 ***   Straight grain.
  ☆   The choice is yours.

Read the Basic Directions (pages 6–11) before starting this project.

Templates A and B are part of diagram 1. Each block requires one A piece and four B pieces, but pay attention; half of B are ties and half are background (diagram 1).

Make a template A. Cut three 2½" strips. You will need 50 A pieces for the ties.

diagram 1

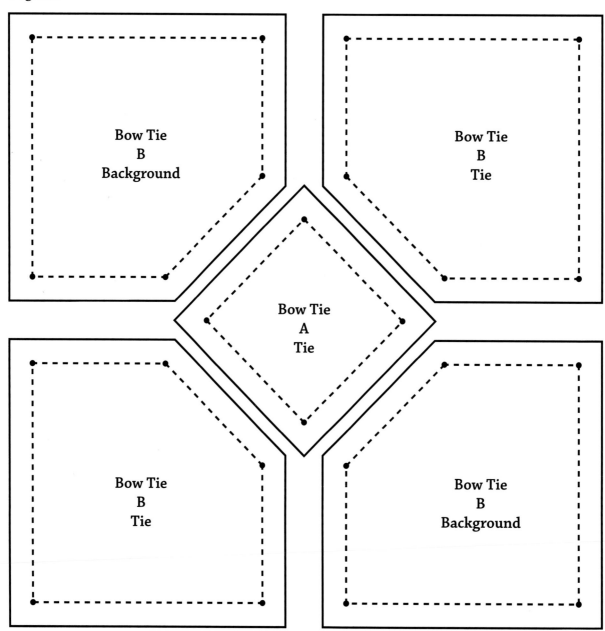

Bow Tie
B
Background

Bow Tie
B
Tie

Bow Tie
A
Tie

Bow Tie
B
Tie

Bow Tie
B
Background

Make a template B. Cut nine 3½" strips. You will need 100 B pieces for the ties.

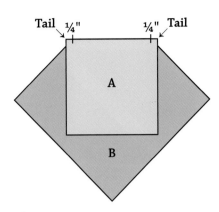

Tail   ¼"   ¼"   Tail

A

B

diagram 2

Arrange the pieces on a flat surface or a design wall to create a pleasing look.

Begin by sewing an A piece to a B piece. There will be a slight tail on each end of A. Stitch starting in ¼" and stop ¼" before the end. Backstitch (diagram 2).

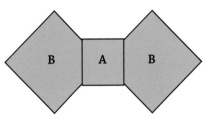

B   A   B

diagram 3

Add another B unit to the other side of A, making sure to stop and start at the ¼" mark. Backstitch. Press the seam toward the center square (diagram 3).

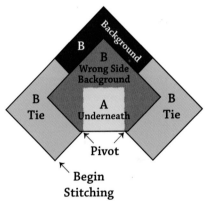

Background

B

B
Wrong Side
Background

B
Tie

A
Underneath

B
Tie

Pivot

Begin
Stitching

diagram 4

To add the first background piece B, start sewing ¼" from the outside edge of the block and stitch to the center square (A). Pivot the needle at the ¼" seam allowance, gently pulling the previously sewn seam allowances out of the way, then stitch along A. Pivot again to sew the final seam (diagram 4).

Repeat for the second background B to complete the block.

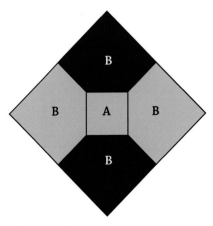

B

B   A   B

B

diagram 5

Press the blocks carefully; I prefer to press the seams toward the center of the block. This technique appears to raise the tie from the surface (diagram 5).

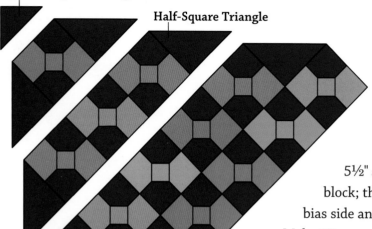

Quarter-Square Triangle

Half-Square Triangle

diagram 6

In the sample quilt, the blocks were set on point. The top was squared off with half-square and quarter-square triangles (diagram 6).

To make 2 half-square triangles, cut a 5½" square and draw a diagonal line across the block; this will be the sewing line. Add a ¼" to the bias side and cut. Discard the other part of the block. Make 17 more (diagram 7).

Cut a 6¼" square and draw 2 diagonal lines to make quarter square triangles (diagram 8).

Press, baste, and quilt. See page 12 photo for quilting ideas.

For the flat piping (flange), measure around the quilt, then cut 1" wide strips to length (plus seam allowances if you must piece these strips together), press in half lengthwise, wrong sides together, and sew the flange to the edge of the quilt with a ⅛" seam before adding the binding.

Use your favorite binding method. Sew on a sleeve and a quilt label.

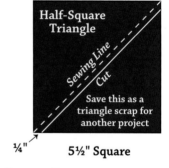

Half-Square Triangle

Sewing Line

Cut

Save this as a triangle scrap for another project

¼" **5½" Square**

diagram 7

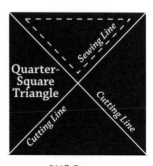

Quarter-Square Triangle

Sewing Line

Cutting Line *Cutting Line*

6¼" Square

diagram 8

GALLERY

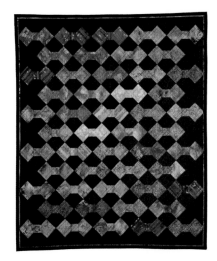

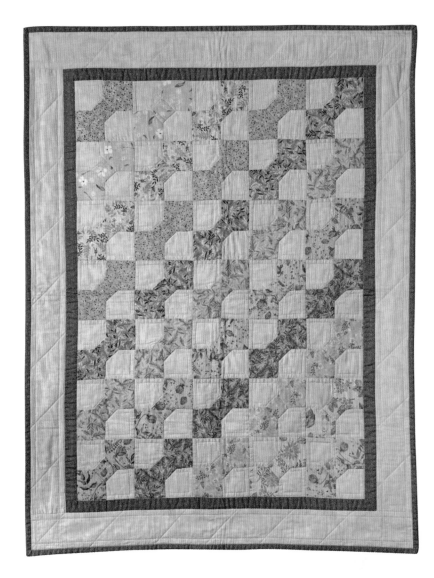

ABOVE: BOW TIE, 36¼" x 42½". Made by Margrette Carr, San Diego, California.

RIGHT: BOW TIE, 32" x 42". Made by Judy Klein, Queens, New York.

BELOW: BOW TIE, 70" x 72", detail. Antique quilt top in the collection of the author.

CARD TRICK

Made by Madalene Becker
Edgewater, Colorado
(See page 22)

Madalene used her collection of fruit and vegetable fabrics to make this quilt for her kitchen. She also turned the border to the back to create her binding. If you choose to do this, add the binding yardage to the border yardage.

Block Size	Sample Quilt	Twin	Queen
12" finished	56" x 56"	72" x 96"	84" x 96"
Fabric (yards)			
5 colors for cards and background	1½ each	1 each	1¼ each
Sashing	2½	☆	☆
Border	1¾ (4" x 56")	☆	☆
Backing	3	4¾	8¾
Binding*	½	¾	¾
Construction			
Block arrangement	3 x 3	6 x 8	7 x 8
Total blocks	9	42	56

*   Straight grain.
☆   The choice is yours.

• •

Read the Basic Directions (pages 6–11) before starting this project.

Diagrams 1a and 1b include the templates for A and B.

Make a template for A and cut fabric into ten 5" strips. You will need 108 A pieces.

Make a template for B and cut fabric into eight 3¼" strips. You will need 108 B pieces.

Arrange your pieces on a flat surface or a design wall to create a pleasing look and check the placement to visualize the "cards."

Sew 2 A pieces together and finger press (diagram 1a), then sew 3 more units.

Tips:

○ **If you use the outer border fabric in the card blocks as Madalene did, cut border strips first.**

○ **When cutting B pieces, place the long side on the straight grain of fabric.**

○ **Measure the quilt top before cutting border strips.**

diagram 1a

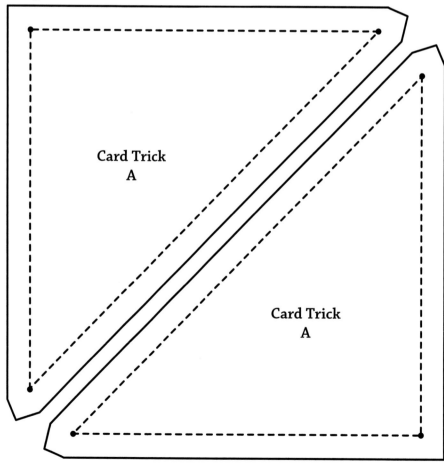

Card Trick
A

Card Trick
A

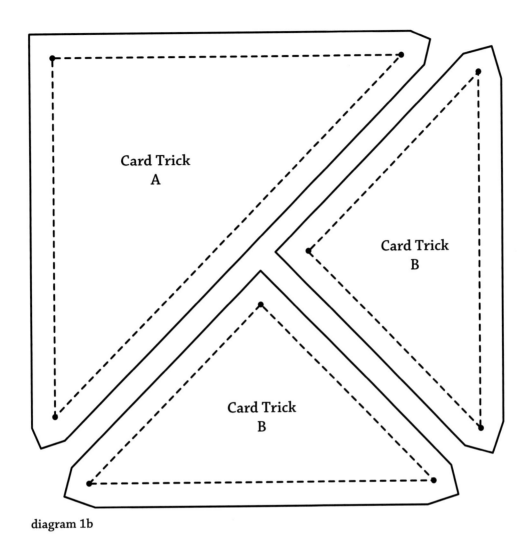

diagram 1b

Sew 2 B pieces together and finger press. Pin the B unit to the long side of an A piece and stitch. Finger press the block flat (diagram 1b), then sew 3 more units.

Sew 4 B pieces together and finger press (diagram 2). Make 1.

Sew these 9 units together to create 1 block (diagram 2).

Your block should measure 12½". If it doesn't, check your ¼" seam and make adjustments.

Make 8 more blocks. Press them all lightly.

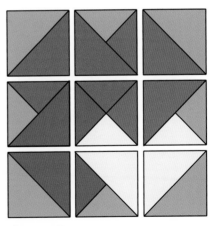

diagram 2

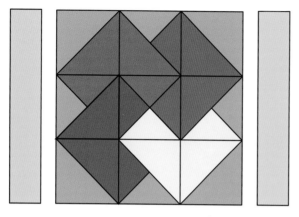

diagram 3

Cut 24 sashing strips 3" x 12½". Sew 12 of them to the sides of each block (diagram 3). Sew the blocks into 3 rows.

Cut 16 squares 3". Sew a sashing/square unit of 4 squares and 3 sashing strips (diagram 4). Make 4.

Using the quilt photo as a reference, attach these sashing/square units to the block/strip units. Be careful to match all of the seams.

diagram 4

Cut 2 border strips 4½" x 46". Cut 2 border strips 4½" x 54½" (diagram 4). Attach these to the sides, top, and bottom.

Press, baste, and quilt. Use your favorite binding method. Sew on a sleeve and a quilt label.

LEFT: CARD TRICK, 56" x 56". Made by Madalene Becker, Edgewater, Colorado.

GALLERY

ABOVE: CARD TRICK, 44" x 62". Made by the author.

ABOVE RIGHT: CARD TRICK, 32" x 32". Made by Linda Denner, Warrensburg, New York.

RIGHT: CARD TRICK SOLUTIONS, 28" x 36". Made by Margrette Carr, San Diego, California.

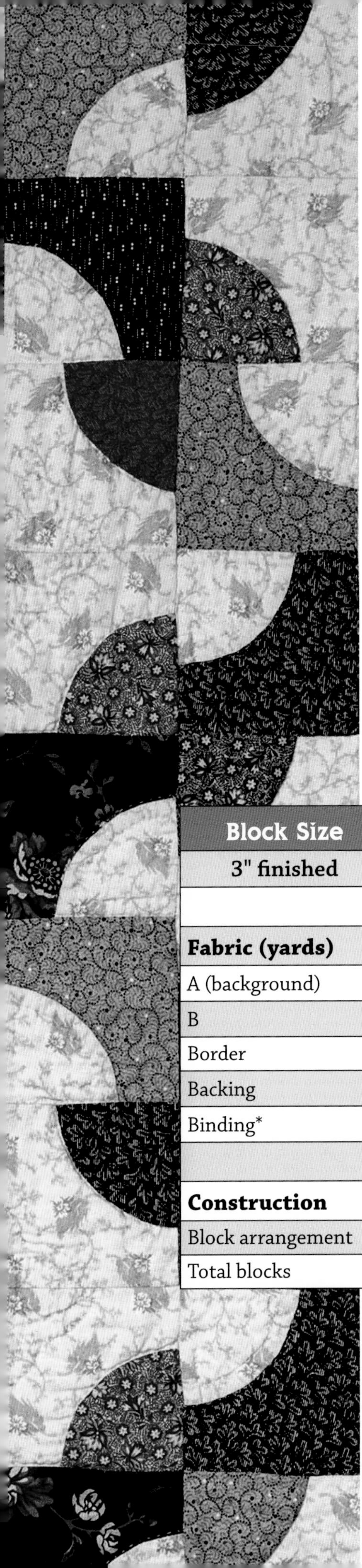

DRUNKARD'S PATH

Made by Doris Salmon
Pilesgrove, New Jersey
(See page 27)

Doris used the same background fabric (piece A) in every block. A scrappy choice would also look great.

Block Size	Sample Quilt	Twin	Queen
3" finished	31½" x 34½"	63" x 87"	84" x 93"
Fabric (yards)			
A (background)	¾	2¾	4
B	¾	2¾	4
Border	1	☆	☆
Backing	1¼	5	☆
Binding*	¼	½	☆
Construction			
Block arrangement	9 x 10	21 x 29	28 x 31
Total blocks	90	609	868

* Straight grain.
☆ The choice is yours.

Read the Basic Directions (pages 6-11) before starting this project.

Templates A and B are in diagram 1.

Make a template for A and cut fabric into ten 4" strips, 5 of each color. In the sample quilt, all of the background (A) pieces were cut from the same light fabric. If you choose to use 1 background fabric, you will need 90 pieces. If you prefer a scrappier look, you will need 45 light and 45 dark A pieces.

Make a template for B and cut fabric into eight 3" strips, 4 of each color. In the sample quilt, the B pieces were cut from various dark fabrics. If you choose this option, you will need 90 pieces. If you prefer a scrappier look, you will need 45 light and 45 dark B pieces.

To piece a Drunkard's Path unit, fold A in half and finger press. Then fold B in half and finger press (diagram 1).

Tips:

⦿ Sometimes I use a stiletto to maintain the raw edge alignment to the block.

⦿ I like to have piece B on the top.

⦿ If the block is not lying flat, clip every ¼" into the curved edge seam allowance of Piece A cutting up to but not into the seam allowance, perpendicular to the raw edge.

diagram 1

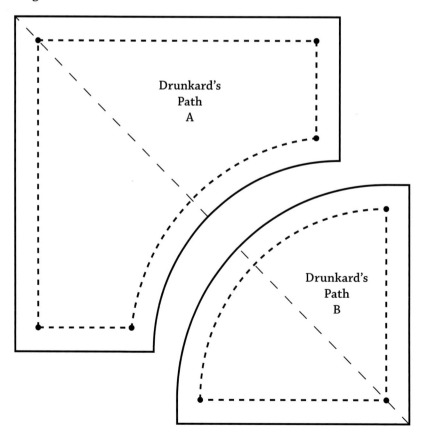

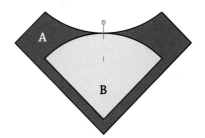

diagram 2

With a pin, match the center folds (diagram 2), right sides together.

Keeping the edges even, pin from the center out to the right and then to the left (diagram 3).

Stitch a ¼" seam edge to edge (diagram 4). Make 89 more units.

This pattern has hundreds of design possibilities! Choose one that is pleasing to you.

Arrange the pieces on a flat surface or a design wall. Pay attention that you have cut an equal number of dark and light pieces of each shape. Sew the Drunkard's Path units together (diagram 4).

Piece the blocks in rows first and then sew the rows together to make the top (diagram 5).

Measure your top through the center vertically and cut 2 borders 2½" x that measurement (the sample quilt was 29½") and sew to the 2 sides.

Measure your top horizontally through the center and cut 2 borders 2½" x that measurement (the sample quilt was 30½") and sew to the top and bottom.

Press, baste, and quilt. Use your favorite binding method. Sew on a sleeve and a quilt label.

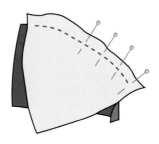

diagram 3

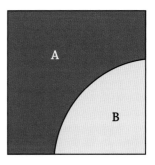

diagram 4

GALLERY

BELOW: DRUNKARD'S PATH, 32" x 35", detail photo pages 2–3. Made by Rita Rehm, Hebron, Connecticut.

ABOVE: DRUNKARD'S PATH, 31½" x 34½". Made by Doris Salmon, Pilesgrove, New Jersey.

diagram 5

ENVELOPE

Made by Linda Denner
Warrensburg, New York
(See page 33)

Linda reversed the colors for the envelopes and flaps using an assortment of light and dark prints.

Block Size	Sample Quilt	Twin	Queen
5½" x 8" finished	34" x 39"	66" x 88"	88" x 96"
Fabric (yards)			
Assorted scraps	1¼	5¼	10
Sashing	1	☆	☆
Outer border	1¼	☆	☆
Backing	1¼	5	8¾
Binding*	¼	½	¾
Construction			
Block arrangement	3 x 5	11 x 11	16 x 12
Total blocks	15	121	192

* Straight grain.
☆ The choice is yours.

· ·

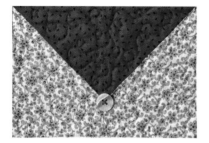

Read the Basic Directions (pages 6–11) before starting this project.

Templates A, AR, B, and BR are in diagrams 1a and 1b.

Make 1 template A/AR and cut flap fabric into three 5" strips. You will need 15 A pieces and 15 AR pieces.

Make 1 template B/BR and cut envelope fabric into four 6½" strips. You will need 15 B and 15 BR pieces.

Arrange your pieces on a flat surface or a design wall to create a pleasing look.

diagram 1a

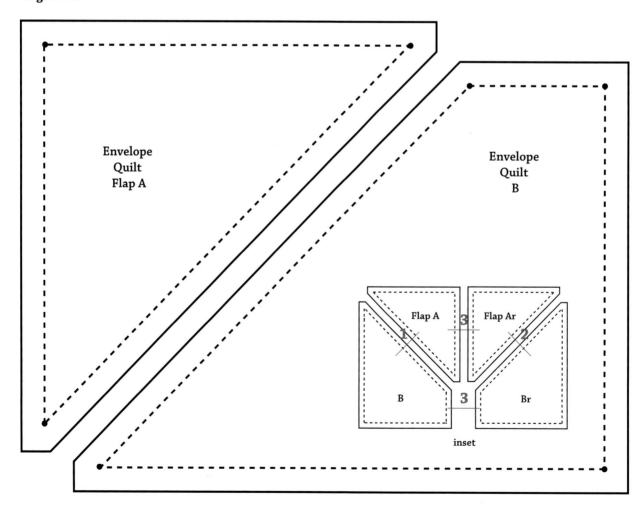

Envelope Quilt Flap A

Envelope Quilt B

Flap A 3 Flap Ar

1 2

B 3 Br

inset

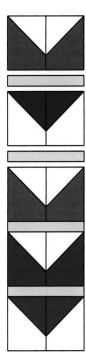

Stitch an A to a B (1), an AR to a BR (2), and then stitch those two units together (3) (diagram 1a inset).

Make 14 more units. Press.

Cut 12 block sashing strips 1½" x 8½". Sew the sashing strips to the blocks (diagram 2).

diagram 2

diagram 1b

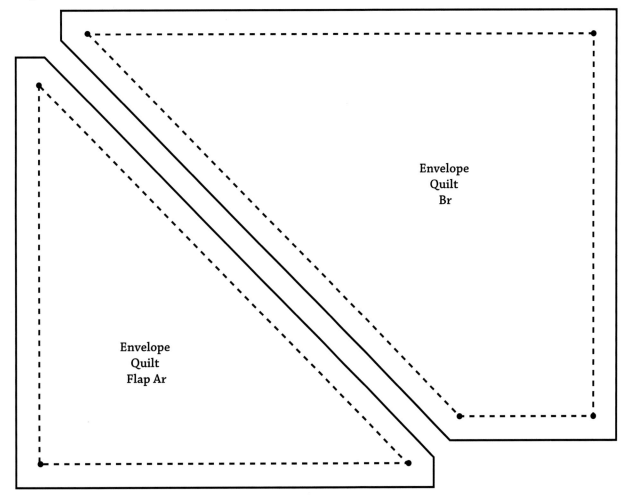

Envelope
Quilt
Br

Envelope
Quilt
Flap Ar

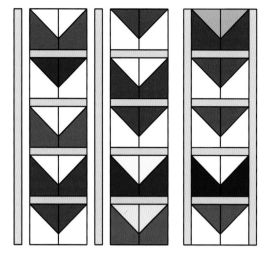

diagram 3

diagram 4

diagram 5

Cut 4 vertical sashing strips 1½" x 30½". Attach to the rows (diagram 3).

Cut 2 horizontal sashing strips 1½" x 27½". Attach to the top and bottom (diagram 4).

Cut 2 border strips 3¾" x 32½". Attach them to the 2 sides (diagram 4).

Cut 2 border strips 3¾" x 34½". Attach them to the top and bottom (diagram 5). Press.

Baste, quilt, and bind. Sew on a sleeve and a quilt label.

For a little extra special touch, sew a button to each envelope flap after quilting

Tips:

○ It is best to measure your top through the center before cutting long sashing or border strips so your quilt will lie flat.

○ I like to attach long side borders starting at the top on one side and then turn the quilt and attach the other border from bottom to top. This will prevent the borders from stretching.

GALLERY

ABOVE: ENVELOPE, 29½" x 31½". Made by Claudia Olinkiewicz, Shelter Island Heights, New York.

LEFT: ENVELOPE, 34" x 39". Made by Linda Denner, Warrensburg, New York.

FLYING GEESE

Made by Dorothy Graves
West Hartford, Connecticut
(See page 37)

This two-patch block is a wonderful use of your small scraps. Dorothy used a striped print for the border and the sashing. If you choose to do the same, you will need extra yardage. The amount will depend on the stripe repeat in the fabric.

Block Size	Sample Quilt	Twin	Queen
3" x 6" finished	27½" x 34½"	66" x 87"	84" x 93"
Fabric (yards)			
A (Triangle)	1	2½	3½
B (Triangle)	1	2½	3½
Sashing/border	1 (2¼" x 34½")	☆	☆
Backing	1	5	4¾
Binding*	¼	½	¾
Construction			
Block arrangement	3 x 10	11 x 29	14 x 31
Total blocks	30	319	434

* Straight grain.

☆ The choice is yours.

Read the Basic Directions (pages 6–11) before starting this project.

Templates A and B are in diagram 1.

diagram 1

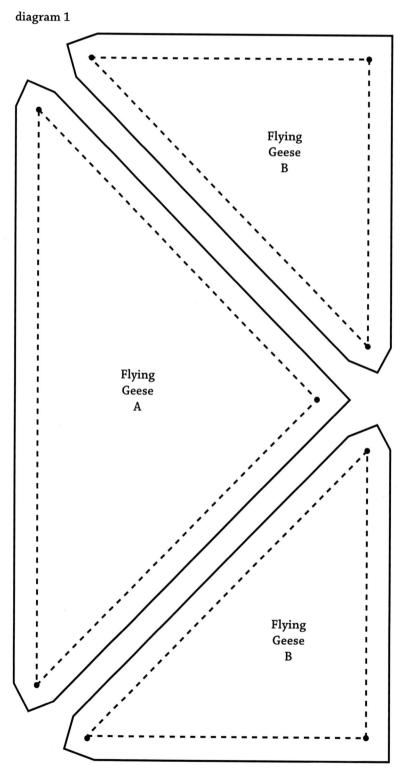

Flying
Geese
B

Flying
Geese
A

Flying
Geese
B

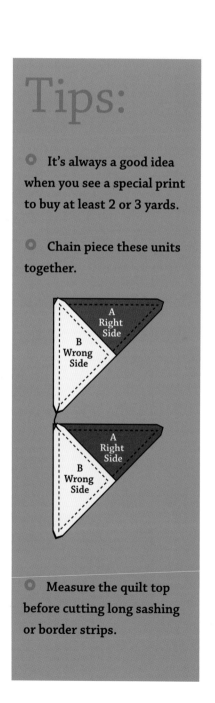

Make a template for A. Cut fabric into seven 4¼" strips. You will need 30 A pieces.

Make a template for B and cut fabric into seven 4" strips. You will need 60 B pieces.

Arrange your pieces on a flat surface or a design wall to create a pleasing look.

Begin by sewing a B piece to either side of 1 A piece edge to edge (diagram 1).

Sew 30 units. Sew the geese units together (diagram 2).

Make 3 vertical columns of 10.

Cut 2 sashing strips 2¾" x 30½" and stitch them to join the 3 columns together (diagram 3).

Cut 2 border strips 2¾" x 27½" sew them to the top and bottom of the quilt.

Cut 2 border strips 2¾" x 34½" sew them to the sides of the quilt.

Miter the corners (see page 10).

Press, baste, and quilt. Use your favorite binding method. Sew on a sleeve and a quilt label.

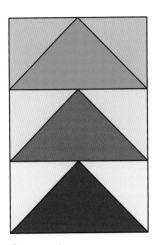

diagram 2

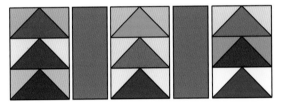

diagram 3

BELOW: FLYING GEESE, 27½" x 34½". Made by Dorothy Graves, West Hartford, Connecticut.

GOLDEN CIRCLE STAR

Made by Betsy O'Neill
Tavares, Florida
(See page 42)

This is an old Kansas City Star pattern first published in 1937. Can't you just imagine the colorful stars made from flour and feed sacks? Betsy used her collection of batiks for a very modern look.

Block Size	Sample Quilt	Twin	Queen
11" finished	40" x 47"	66" x 88"	88" x 99"
Fabric (yards)			
A (Prism)	2¾	6¼	8¾
B (Star)	(assorted scraps) total	(assorted scraps) total	(assorted scraps) total
B (Background)	for all As and Bs	for all As and Bs	for all As and Bs
Inner border (½")	1½	☆	☆
Outer border (3")	1½	☆	☆
Backing	1½	5	8¾
Binding*	¼	½	¾
Construction			
Block arrangement	4 x 5	6 x 8	8 x 9
Full blocks	20	48	72

*   Straight grain.

☆   The choice is yours.

Read the Basic Directions (pages 6–11) before starting this project.

Make a template A from diagram 1, which also shows a cutting plan. Cut eleven 3" strips on the bias and then cut the prism piece. You will need 63 A pieces.

Make a template B from diagram 2. Cut fabric into twenty 2¾" strips. You will need 240 diamonds.

Arrange your pieces on a flat surface or a design wall to create a pleasing look.

Piece 3 diamonds (B) together as shown in diagram 2. Sew 3 more diamonds together.

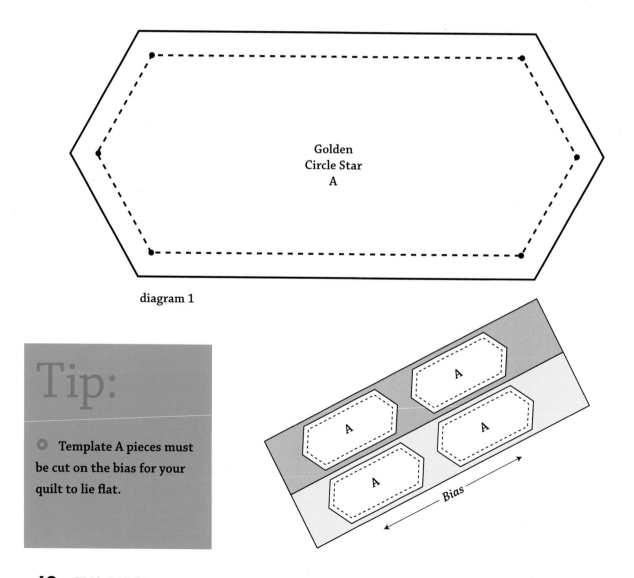

Golden
Circle Star
A

diagram 1

Tip:

○ Template A pieces must be cut on the bias for your quilt to lie flat.

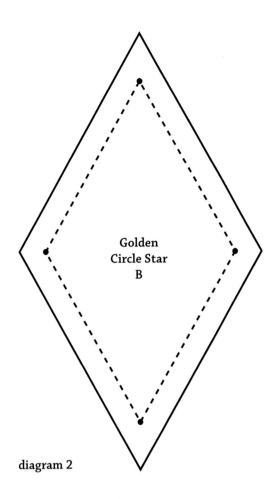

Golden
Circle Star
B

diagram 2

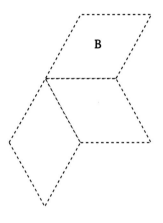

B

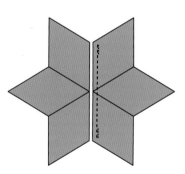

diagram 3

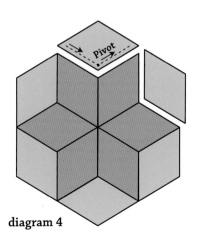

Pivot

diagram 4

With right sides together, match the center point of these 2 units with a pin. Two seams will go to the right and 2 to the left. Pin across the seam, being careful not to stretch the diamonds. Begin stitching ¼" in from the edge and backstitch. Sew to ¼" from the end. Backstitch (diagram 3).

With your finger, press the center seams into a swirl on the back so that the seams will lie flat.

Next, stitch 6 background diamonds (B) to the star to create a hexagon. Stitch from one outside edge to the center, pivot, and stitch to the next outside edge (diagram 4).

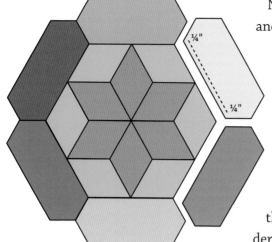

diagram 5

BELOW: GOLDEN CIRCLE STAR, 40" x 47". Made by Betsy O'Neill, Tavares, Florida.

Now attach the prisms around only one hexagon, starting and stopping ¼" from the edge (diagram 5).

Refer to the sample quilt photo to continue attaching hexagons and prisms. Betsy created a straight edge for her top by cutting through diamonds and prisms with a long ruler.

Measure through the center of your quilt vertically and add 2 borders 1½" wide to the sides. Measure through the center of your quilt horizontally and add 2 more 1½" borders to the top and bottom.

Add another border 3" wide in the same manner.

Press, baste, and quilt. Use your favorite binding method. Sew on a sleeve and a quilt label.

HUMMINGBIRD

Author's Antique Collection
(See page 110)

This quilt gave me the motivation and idea to create this two patch book; it is one of my favorite quilt tops. Imagine the women's dresses, men's shirts, aprons, and scraps from the sewing box of the late 1800s that were the source of these small pieces. The black-and-white shirting fabric connects all of the stars together.

Block Size	Sample Quilt	Twin	Queen
6" finished	66" x 72"	66" x 90"	84" x 96"
Fabric (yards)			
A (Hummingbird); light and dark mediums	4¼ (assorted lights) 4¼ (assorted darks)	4½ (assorted lights) 4½ (assorted darks)	5¾ (assorted lights) 5¾ (assorted darks)
B (Background); lights			
Backing	4¼	4¼	8¾
Binding*	1¼	1¼	1¼
Construction			
Block arrangement	15 x 18	11 x 15	14 x 16
Total blocks	270	165	224

* Straight grain.

• •

Read the Basic Directions (pages 6-11) before starting this project.

Template A is in the cutting chart shown in diagram 1. Template B is in the cutting chart shown in diagram 2.

For A pieces, cut fabric into ninety 4" strips. You will need 1080 A pieces.

For B pieces, cut fabric into ninety 3" strips. You will need 1080 B pieces.

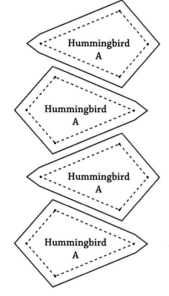

Cutting diagram for Template A

diagram 1

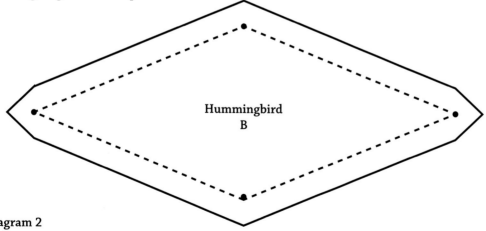

diagram 2

Cutting diagram for Template B

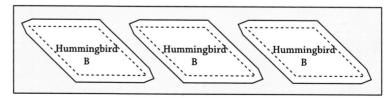

Arrange your pieces on a flat surface or a design wall to create a pleasing look.

Join medium light and dark A prints in pairs (diagram 3).

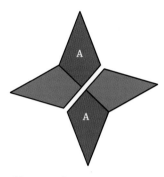

diagram 3

Join the pairs together to create a star unit. Make 269 more star units (diagram 4).

Arrange 15 star units across and 18 star units down. Begin joining stars into rows with the B shape (diagram 5).

Continue joining rows (diagrams 6 and 7).

The outside edge of my antique top was pieced with B (the diamond shape) which was then cut in half to square the outside edge.

This is one of many antique quilt tops in my collection yet to be quilted (see detail page 43).

diagram 4

BELOW: AMERICA THE BEAUTIFUL, 29" x 35". Made by Rene Williams, Northridge, California.

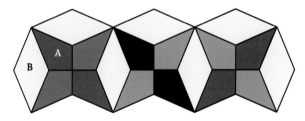

diagram 5

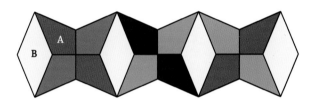

diagram 6

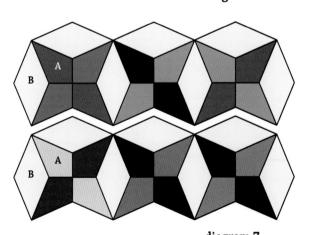

diagram 7

JOSEPH'S COAT

Made by Mary Shurpik
Stony Brook, New York
(See page 49)

Mary used a variety of scraps with lots of light, medium, and dark prints. She used a collection of dark fabrics to border the quilt. Then she used scrap triangles on the two sides to square up the quilt.

Block Size	Sample Quilt	Twin	Queen
6" finished	30" x 35"	66" x 90"	84" x 96"
Fabric (yards)			
A (Triangle)	2½ for A and B	4¼ for A and B	5¾ for A and B
B (Melon)	1 for B		
Backing	1	5	8¾
Binding*	¼	½	¾
Construction			
Block arrangement	5 x 5	11 x 15	14 x 16
Total blocks	23	165	224
Half blocks	4	☆	☆

* Straight grain.

☆ The choice is yours.

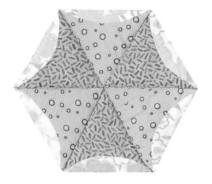

With the A shape you need to use a 28mm rotary cutter.

Read the Basic Directions (pages 6–11) before starting this project.

Make a template for A and B and mark the center line (diagram 1).

For A pieces, cut fabric into twenty 4" strips. You will need 150 pieces for the blocks plus 54 for the outer border.

For B pieces, cut fabric into twenty 1½" strips. You will need 184 pieces.

This pattern requires some design work ahead of time. Arrange your pieces on a flat surface or a design wall to create a pleasing look.

To stitch, fold both shapes in half to find the center. I like to have the melon piece (B) on the top (diagram 2). Pin in the center, and pin to the left and to the right. Using a ¼" seam, begin stitching at the edge and sew across, easing in the melon. Finger press the seam toward A. Sew 5 more units together (diagram 3).

diagram 1

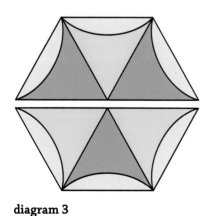

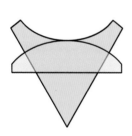

diagram 2

diagram 3

Joseph's
Coat
A

Joseph's
Coat
B

See page 47 about how Mary created her border.

Press, baste, quilt, and bind. Sew on a sleeve and a quilt label.

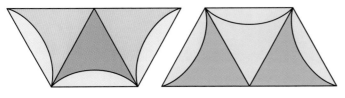

diagram 4

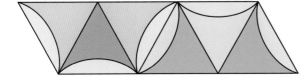

diagram 5

GALLERY

Tips:

○ Pin and sew the joined units of triangles and melons together in a row to avoid creating Y seams as you join the blocks (diagram 4). Diagram 5 is a completed row.

○ Use a size 14 needle when quilting to get through the intersections.

○ Mary used left over scraps on the back of her quilt...Not to waste a scrap!

ABOVE: JOSEPH'S COLOR WHEEL, 33" x 34". Made by Mary Shurpik, Stony Brook, New York.

RIGHT TOP: JOSEPH'S COLOR WHEEL, back.

RIGHT: JOSEPH'S COAT, 30" x 35". Made by Mary Shurpik, Stony Brook, New York.

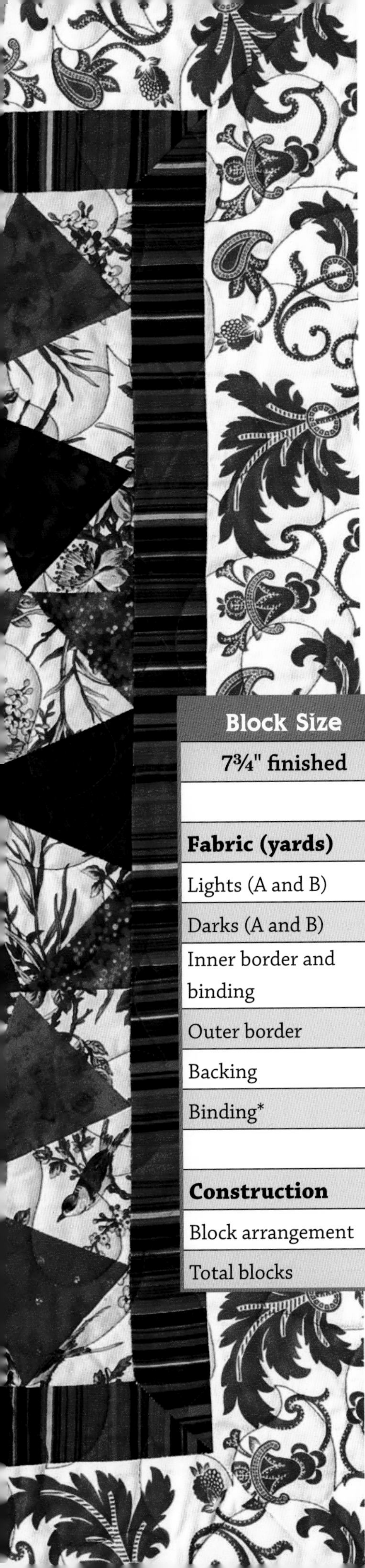

KALEIDOSCOPE

Made by Sylvia A. Frontz
El Cajon, California
(See page 53)

To frame the many medium red print scraps and one background fabric, Sylvia used a striped fabric to accent her mitered inner border.

Block Size	Sample Quilt	Twin	Queen
7¾" finished	35½" x 35½"	64" x 88"	88" x 96"
Fabric (yards)			
Lights (A and B)	½	2¼	3¼
Darks (A and B)	½	2¼	3¼
Inner border and binding	¾	☆	☆
Outer border	1¼	☆	☆
Backing	1	5	8¾
Binding*	¼	½	¾
Construction			
Block arrangement	3 x 3	8 x 11	11 x 12
Total blocks	9	88	132

* Straight grain.
☆ The choice is yours.

Read the Basic Directions (pages 6–11) before starting this project.

Diagram 1 shows template A and a cutting plan. Make a template for A and cut light and dark fabrics into seven 5" strips. You will need 36 light and 36 dark triangles.

Make a template for B (diagram 2) and cut fabric into twelve 3" strips. You will need 20 light and 16 dark triangles.

Tips:

○ When cutting the small triangles, lay the short sides of the triangle on the straight grain of the fabric (diagram 1).

○ When joining the four large triangles to each other, find the center and finger press two seams to the left and the other set to the right. Find the center of the block and pin, placing pins to the left and right of the block. Before sewing, remove the center pin and you will always match at the center!

○ Press the center seam open to minimize bulk in the block.

○ Measure your top before cutting and sewing borders.

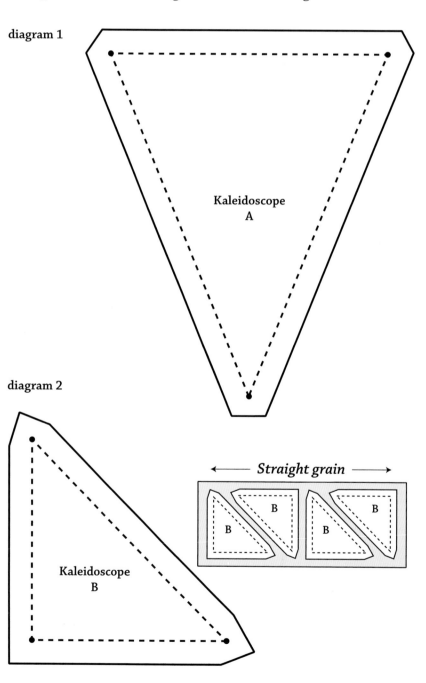

diagram 1

Kaleidoscope
A

diagram 2

Kaleidoscope
B

Straight grain

B B B B B B

Arrange your pieces on a flat surface or a design wall to create a pleasing look. Sew 4 A triangles together in 2 light/dark pairs. Repeat. Sew the 2 units together (diagram 3). Follow the sample quilt photograph for light/dark placement.

Add 4 B triangles to the corners to complete the block (diagram 4).

Follow the sample quilt photograph to create the alternate block arrangement.

For the inner border cut 4 pieces 2" x 25". Stitch them first to the sides and then to the top and bottom.

For the outer border cut 4 pieces 5" x 35". Stitch to the top and bottom and then to the 2 sides.

Press, baste, and quilt. Use your favorite binding method. Sew on a sleeve and a quilt label.

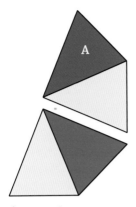

diagram 3

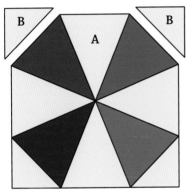

diagram 4

LEFT: KALEIDOSCOPE, 35½" x 35½". Made by Sylvia A. Frontz, El Cajon, California.

KALEIDOSCOPE

GALLERY

RIGHT: KALEIDOSCOPE I, 42" x 42". Made by the author.

LEFT: KALEIDOSCOPE, 27½" x 27½". Made by Linda Denner, Warrensburg, New York.

LEFT: KALEIDOSCOPE, 40" x 40". Made by Susan Gilmore, Columbia, Missouri. Quilted by Margrette Carr, San Diego, California

RIGHT: KALEIDOSCOPE II, 21" x 21". Made by the author.

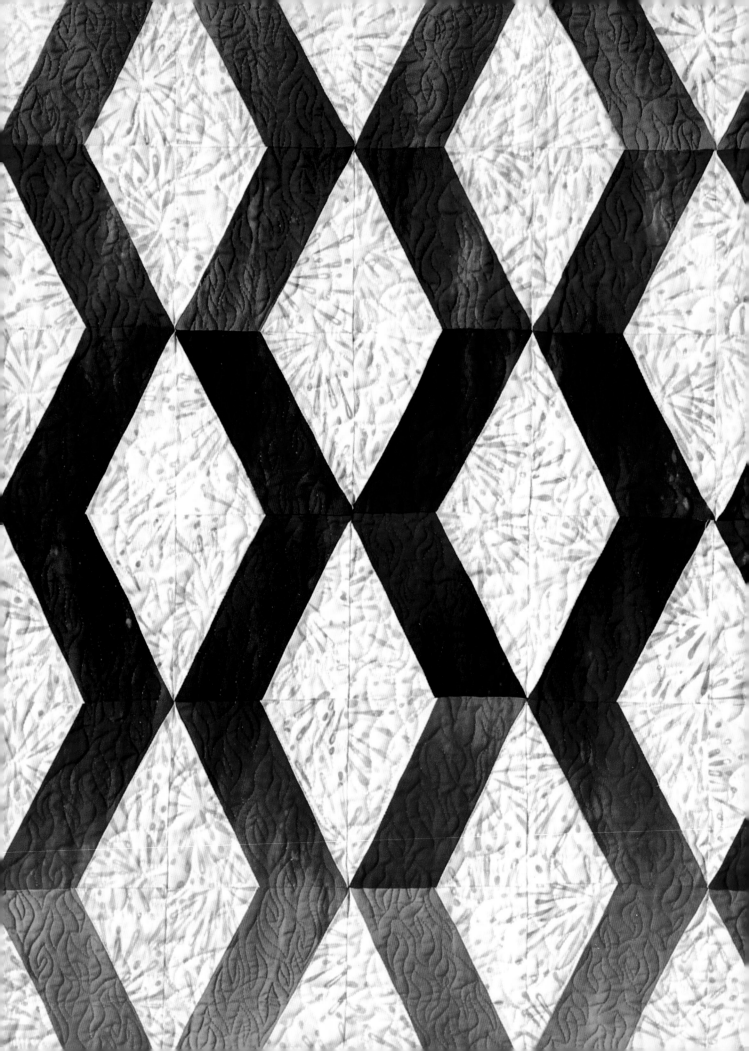

LEFT AND RIGHT

Made by Linda Denner
Warrensburg, New York
(See page 59)

Linda chose a cream color for her background fabric and hand-dyed rainbow fabrics for the defining piece (parallelogram) in the blocks.

Block Size	Sample Quilt	Twin	Queen
8" finished	32" x 40"	64" x 88"	88" x 96"
Fabric (yards)			
A/AR (Background)	1	2¼	3¼
B/BR (Parallelograms)	1 (assorted scraps)	2¼	3¼
Inner border	¼ (¾" finished)	☆	☆
Outer border	1¼ (3½" finished)	☆	☆
Backing	1¼	5	8¾
Binding*	¼	½	¾
Construction			
Block arrangement	6 x 8	8 x 11	11 x 12
Total blocks	48	88	132

* Straight grain.
☆ The choice is yours.

• •

Read the Basic Directions (pages 6–11) before starting this project.

Make a template for A/AR (see page 59). Cut fabric into ten 5" strips. You will need 48 A and 48 AR.

Make a template for B/BR (see page 59). Cut fabric into ten 5" strips. You will need 48 B and 48 BR.

Sew a background shape (A/AR) to either side of the parallelogram (B/BR) (diagrams 1 and 2). Finger press the seams away from the center (diagram 3).

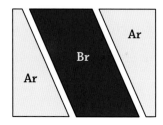

diagram 1

Make 47 more units the same way.

Arrange your pieces on a flat surface or a design wall to create a pleasing look.

To use graduated or shaded fabric like the rainbow fabric for the inner border, cut 2 strips 1¼" x 25" and 2 strips 1¼" x 33" before you cut the fabric for the parallelograms.

When sewing the blocks together, pay attention to the pattern direction to create a zigzag down the quilt. Lots of color arrangements can be made using this pattern. Diagram 4 shows the sample quilt's zigzag arrangement.

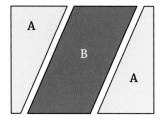

diagram 2

Stitch the top with 6 blocks across and 8 blocks down, matching the seams.

Sew on the inner border, attaching first the 2 side strips and then the top and bottom strips.

Measure your top and cut 2 strips for the outer border 4" x the length. Attach these to the 2 sides. Measure the quilt horizontally and cut 2 strips this width x 4". Attach these to the top and bottom.

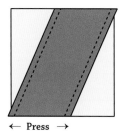

← Press →

diagram 3

Press, baste, and quilt. Use your favorite binding method. Sew on a sleeve and a quilt label.

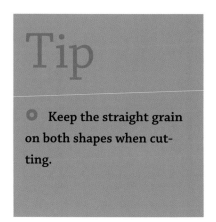

Tip

○ **Keep the straight grain on both shapes when cutting.**

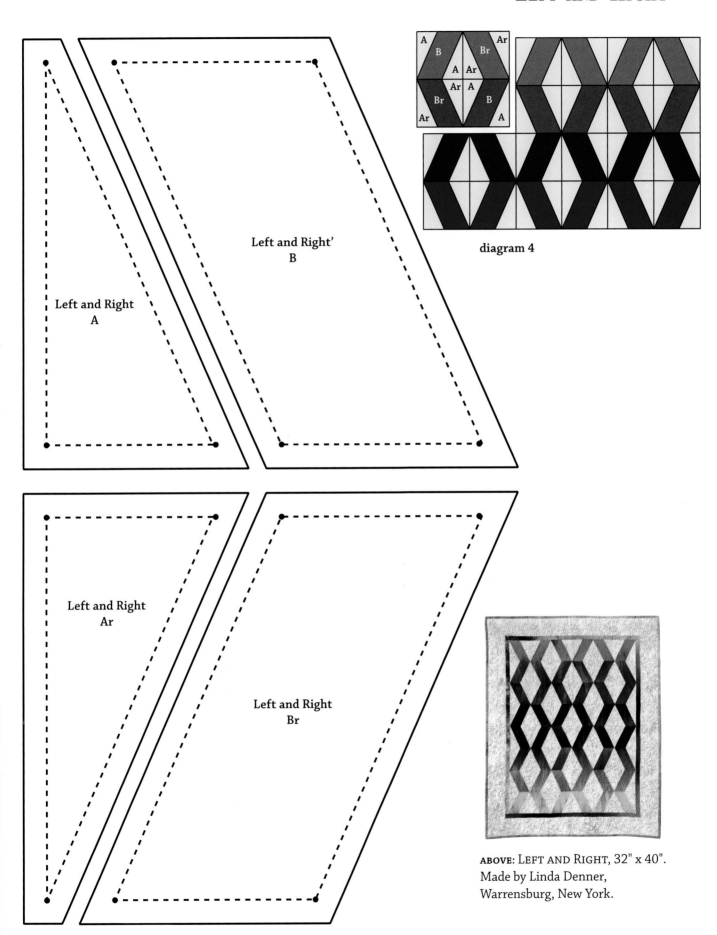

diagram 4

Left and Right
A

Left and Right'
B

Left and Right
Ar

Left and Right
Br

ABOVE: LEFT AND RIGHT, 32" x 40".
Made by Linda Denner,
Warrensburg, New York.

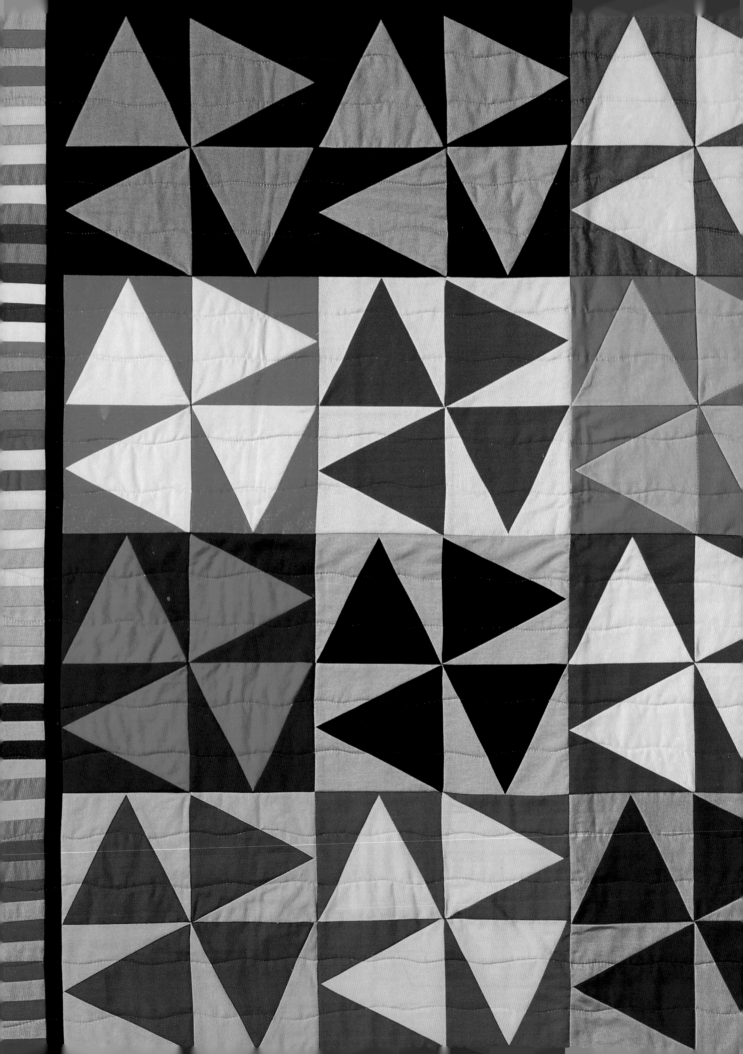

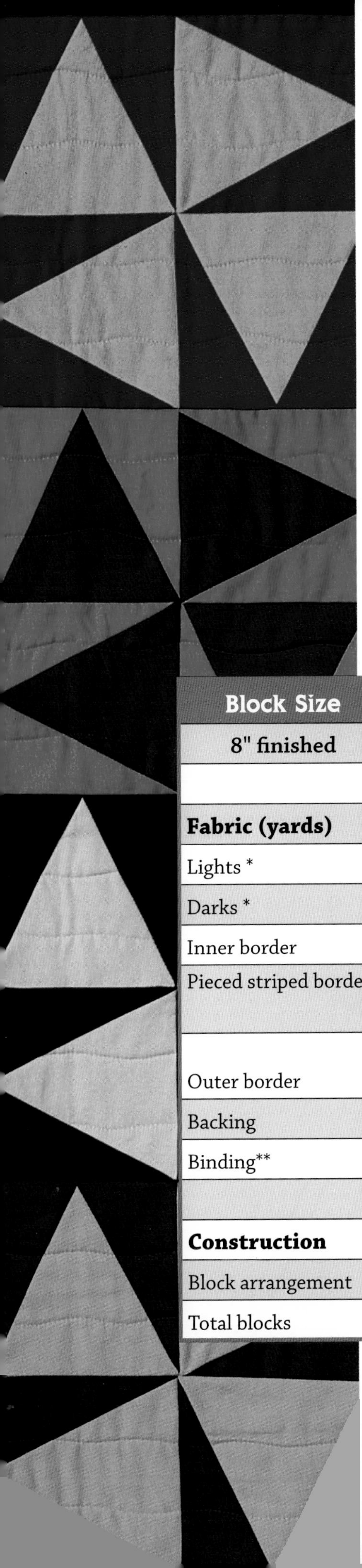

MADALENE'S STAR

Made by Karen Griska
Litchfield, Connecticut
(See page 63)

Karen used her stash of solid color fabrics for this quilt. The pieced border fabrics were cut from the scraps Karen had left over. This border really makes a fabulous frame for the quilt.

Block Size	Sample Quilt	Twin	Queen
8" finished	40" x 40"	64" x 88"	88" x 96"
Fabric (yards)			
Lights *	1	4¼	6
Darks *	1	2½	4
Inner border	½" x 33½" – 1 yard	☆	☆
Pieced striped border	½" x 3" x 40" 1¼ yards	☆	☆
Outer border	4 different colors each ½" x 40"	☆	☆
Backing	1	5	8¾
Binding**	1¼	½	¾
Construction			
Block arrangement	4 x 4	8 x 11	11 x 12
Total blocks	16	88	132

* Study the sample quilt photograph to decide which pieces (A, B, BR) will be light and which will be dark.

** Straight grain.

☆ The choice is yours.

Read the Basic Directions (pages 6-11) before starting this project.

Make a template for A (diagram 1). Cut fabric into six 5" strips. You will need 64 A pieces.

Make a template for B/BR (diagram 1). Cut fabric into six 5" strips. You will need 64 B and 64 BR pieces.

Begin by stitching a BR to an A and then attach a B to the other side of A (diagram 2). Sewing opposite sides of this unit will cause less distortion for the block. Finger press the seams away from the center. Make 3 more units.

Sew 4 units into a block. Pay close attention to the direction of the pattern when attaching the units in the block. Match the points of the block by finding the center and pin. Continue to pin across the block. Stitch. See diagram 3.

Sew 15 more blocks.

diagram 1

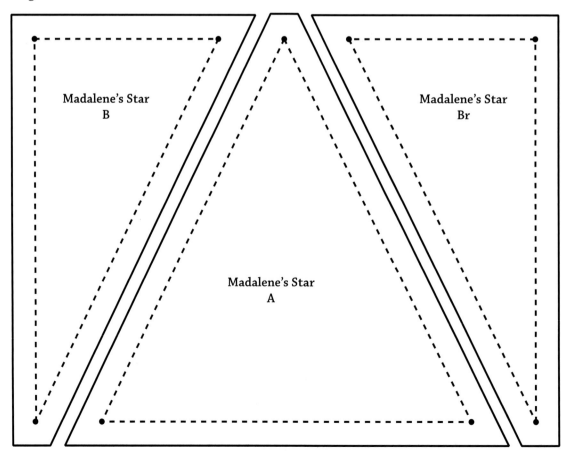

Arrange the blocks on a flat surface or a design wall to create a pleasing look.

Follow the sample quilt photograph to stitch the blocks together in rows and then join the rows. Pay close attention to the seams. Sew one row with the seams all going to the right and the next row all going to the left to avoid bulk.

Measure the quilt top and cut 4 strips 1" x 34½" for the inner border. Attach the top and bottom borders and then stitch on the 2 side borders.

For the pieced border, cut 244 pieces 1" x 3". Piece them together into border strips. Two of the quilt top sides should measure 33½" and 2 should measure 39½". Attach the pieced borders.

Cut 4 pieces for the outer border 1" by 40½". Sew on the outside border.

Press, baste, and quilt. Use your favorite binding method. Sew on a sleeve and a quilt label.

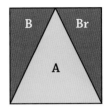

diagram 2

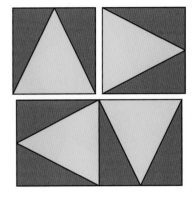

diagram 3

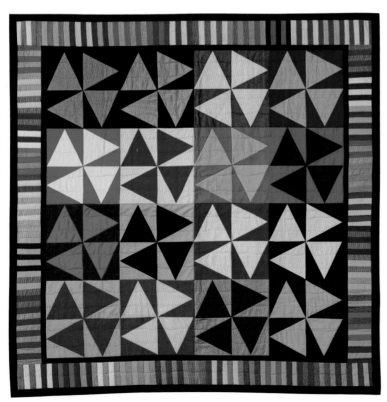

ABOVE: MADALENE'S STAR, 40" x 40". Made by Karen Griska, Litchfield, Connecticut.

Tips:

○ Sewing a ¼" seam is crucial to this pattern because of the angles.

○ Check to make sure the block measures 8½" square. If not, STOP and correct your seam allowance to an accurate ¼". Otherwise, you may be making rectangles instead of squares!

MAGIC SQUARES

Made by Dee Danley-Brown
El Dorado Hills, California
(See page 67)

This is a great scrap quilt for using lots of prints and tone-on-tone solids. Dee's quilt was machine pieced, but it's a great pattern for practicing your hand stitching. She cut a 3" width of black fabric for the border and then appliquéd the outer squares to it. The black is a good choice because it frames the quilt. A colorful binding ties in all of the colors used in the quilt.

Block Size	Sample Quilt	Twin	Queen
3" finished	30" x 33"	63" x 87"	84" x 93"
Fabric (yards)			
A & B	1½ (assorted scraps)	5¼	7½
Border	3" x 33"	☆	☆
Backing	1	5	8¾
Binding*	¼	½	¾
Construction			
Block arrangement	9 x 10	☆	☆
Total A & B pieces	162	☆	☆

* Straight grain.

☆ The choice is yours.

MAGIC SQUARES

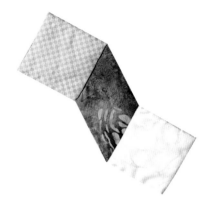

Read the Basic Directions (pages 6–11) before starting this project.

Make a template for A (diagram 1). Cut fabric into ten 3" strips. You will need 72 A pieces.

Make a template for B (diagram 1). Cut fabric into ten 3½" strips. You will need 90 B pieces.

Arrange your pieces on a flat surface or a design wall to create a pleasing look.

diagram 1

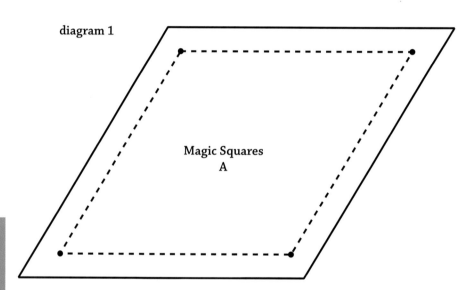

Magic Squares
A

Tips:

○ Start stitching ¼" from the end and stop ¼" before the end, backstitching at both ends to secure the thread.

○ Pay attention to the ¼" seam allowance. You must sew a ¼" seam so the pieces will fit together.

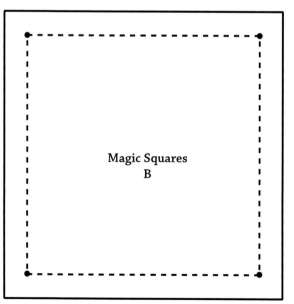

Magic Squares
B

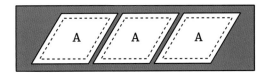

Keep the diamonds in the same direction each time you cut and move them across the strip of fabric (diagram 2).

Pin the diamond to the square; there will be a small end of the diamond showing (diagram 3).

Sew diamonds to squares to make rows (diagram 4).

Sew the rows together. A diamond is always next to a square and vice versa (diagram 5).

The outside edges of the sample quilt top (the squares) were all turned under ¼" and appliquéd down.

Baste, quilt, and bind. Sew on a sleeve and a quilt label.

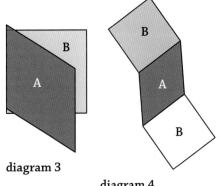

diagram 2

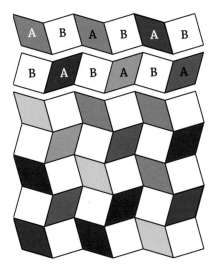

diagram 3

diagram 4

GALLERY

ABOVE: MAGIC SQUARES, 31" x 47". Made by Stevii Graves, Leesburg, Virginia.

RIGHT: MAGIC SQUARES, 30" x 33". Made by Dee Danley-Brown, El Dorado, California.

diagram 5

MARBLE FLOOR

Made by Lynne Williams
Desha, Arkansas
(See page 72)

This pattern can also be made with solid octagons and printed triangles for an entirely different look.

Block Size	Sample Quilt	Twin	Queen
4½" finished	36" x 36"	64" x 85"	85" x 94"
Fabric (yards) *			
A (Octagon) & B (Triangle)	2¼ (assorted scraps)	8¼ (assorted scraps)	11¾ (assorted scraps)
Backing/binding*	1¼	5½	9½
Construction			
Block arrangement	8 x 8	15 x 20	20 x 22
Total blocks	64	300	440

* In the sample quilt, the binding and background fabrics are the same and the backing is different. The yardage given assumes the backing and binding fabric are the same.

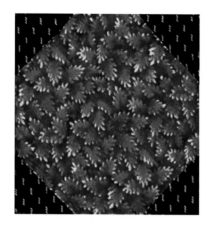

Read the Basic Directions (pages 6-11) before starting this project.

Make a template for A (diagram 1). Cut fabric into twelve 5½" strips. You will need 64 A pieces.

Make a template for B (diagram 1). Cut fabric into eleven 2½" strips. You will need 256 B pieces.

Arrange your pieces on a flat surface or a design wall to create a pleasing look.

diagram 1

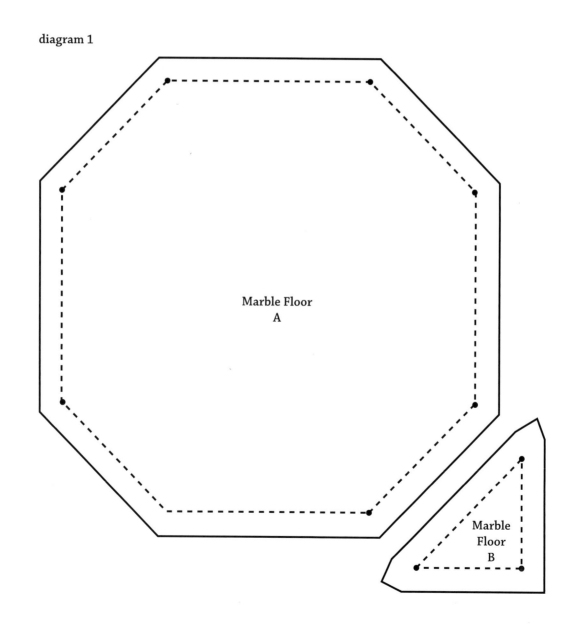

Marble Floor
A

Marble
Floor
B

Sew a B piece to the left corner of an A piece (diagram 2).

Next sew a B piece to the opposite corner (diagram 3).

Finger press the seams away from the center. Attach the other two corners in the same way (diagram 4).

The block should measure 5". If not, adjust your seam allowance.

Make 63 more blocks and lay the blocks out in rows (diagram 5).

Sew the blocks together and then sew the rows together (diagram 6).

Press, baste, and quilt. Sew on your favorite binding. Make a sleeve and a quilt label.

diagram 2

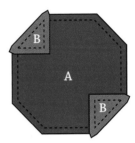

diagram 3

diagram 4

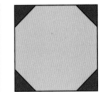

diagram 5

diagram 6

RIGHT: MARBLE FLOOR, 31" x 31".
Made by Kimberley Graf,
San Diego, California.

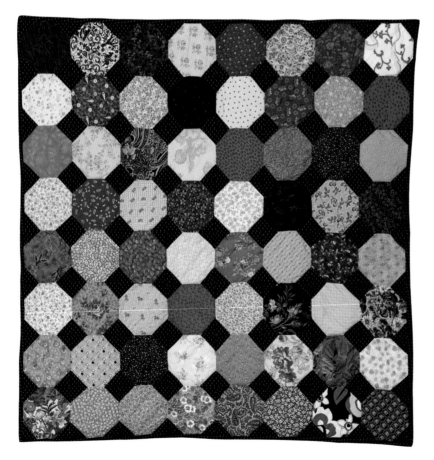

LEFT: MARBLE FLOOR, 36" x 36".
Made by Lynne Williams, Desha,
Arkansas.

MOHAWK TRAIL

Made by Mary Shurpik
Stony Brook, New York
(See page 75)

This pattern has so many design options to try depending on the direction or the position in which the blades are placed in the block settings.

Block Size	Sample Quilt	Twin	Queen
5" finished	40" x 40"	65" x 90"	85" x 95"
Fabric (yards)			
A & B	2 each	6	8
Backing	1¼	5	8¾
Binding*	¼	½	¾
Construction			
Block arrangement	8 x 8	13 x 18	17 x 19
Total blocks	64	234	323

*   Straight grain.

MOHAWK TRAIL

Read the Basic Directions (pages 6–11) before starting this project.

Make a template for A (diagram 1). Cut fabric into eleven 6" strips. You will need 64 A pieces.

Make a template for B (diagram 1). Cut fabric into eleven 5" strips. You will need 192 B pieces.

Arrange the pieces on a flat surface or a design wall to create a pleasing look.

diagram 1

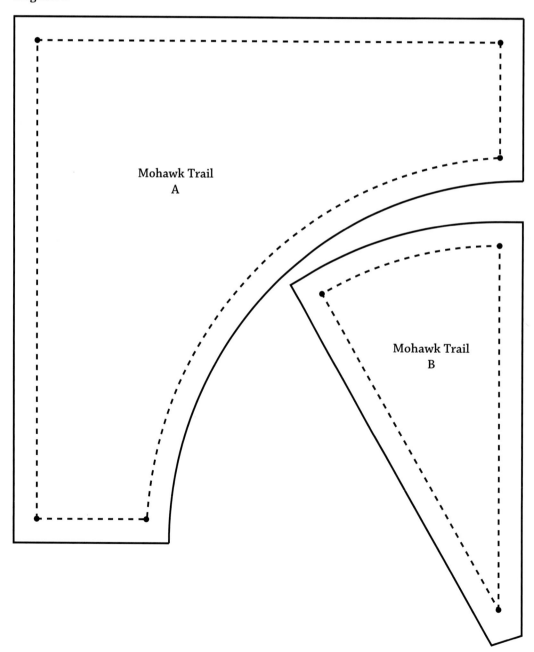

Mohawk Trail
A

Mohawk Trail
B

Begin by sewing 2 Bs together, and then add the 3rd B. Finger press flat (diagram 2).

Fold A in half and finger press to find the center. Fold the B unit in half and finger press to find the center.

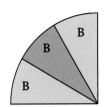

diagram 2

Place the convex piece (B unit) on top of A and match centers with a pin (diagram 3).

Pin to the edge in both directions from the center. Stitch using a ¼" seam. Finger press the seams toward the background (A).

diagram 3

Measure the block. If it is not 5½", adjust your seam allowance. Make 63 more blocks.

Sew the blocks together being careful not to stretch them (diagram 4).

Sew the rows together (diagram 5).

Press, baste, and quilt. Use your favorite binding method. Sew on the sleeve and a quilt label.

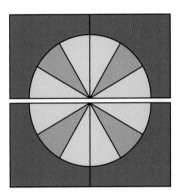

diagram 4

ABOVE: MOHAWK TRAIL, 40" x 40". Made by Mary Shurpik, Stony Brook, New York.

diagram 5

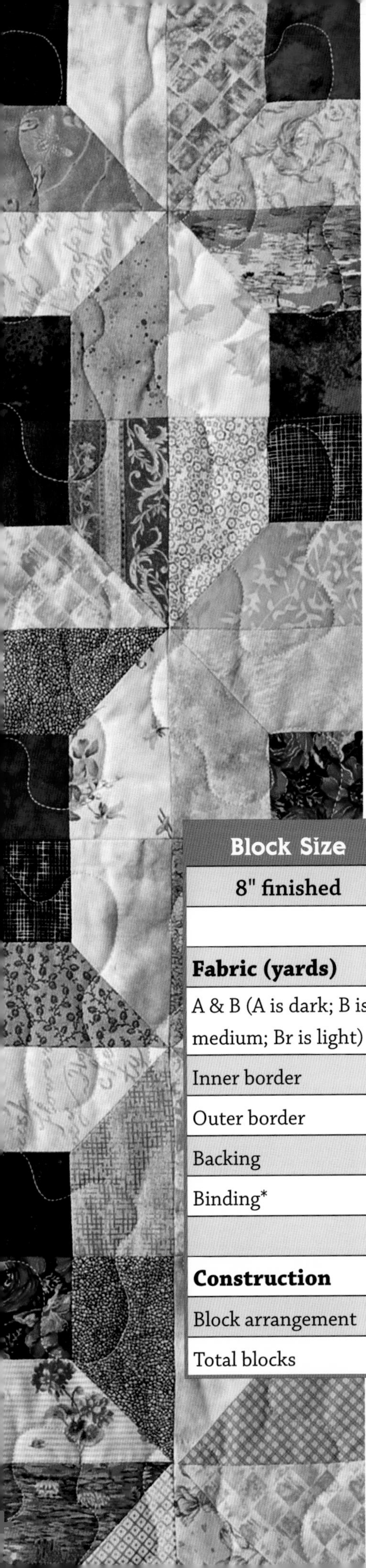

NELSON'S VICTORY

Made by Peggy Weichel
Sorrento, Florida
(See page 79)

This is truly a scrap quilt using a variety of lights, mediums, and darks. Peggy mitered the corners of all of the borders. See mitering directions on page 10 if you like this look and to figure fabric needs. Note that the yardage given here is for butted borders.

Block Size	Sample Quilt	Twin	Queen
8" finished	38½" x 38½"	64" x 88"	88" x 96"
Fabric (yards)			
A & B (A is dark; B is medium; Br is light)	1¼ total (lights, mediums, & darks)	5¾	8¼
Inner border	1	☆	☆
Outer border	1¼	☆	☆
Backing	1¼	5	8¾
Binding*	¼	½	¾
Construction			
Block arrangement	4 x 4	8 x 11	11 x 12
Total blocks	16	88	132

* Straight grain.
☆ The choice is yours.

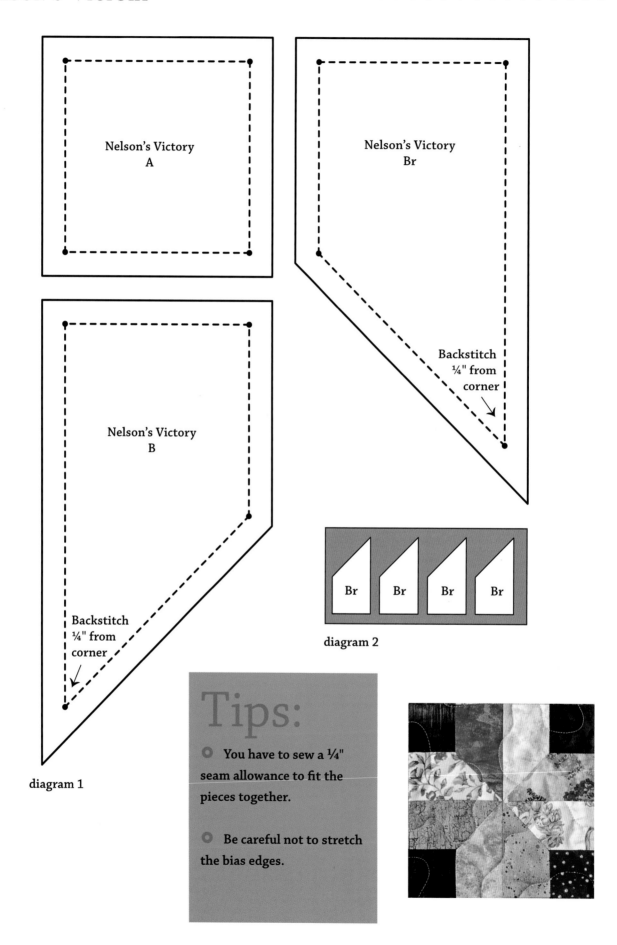

Nelson's Victory
A

Nelson's Victory
Br

Nelson's Victory
B

Backstitch
¼" from
corner

Backstitch
¼" from
corner

diagram 1

| Br | Br | Br | Br |

diagram 2

Tips:

○ You have to sew a ¼"
seam allowance to fit the
pieces together.

○ Be careful not to stretch
the bias edges.

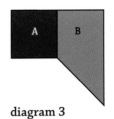

diagram 3

Read the Basic Directions (pages 6-11) before starting this project.

Make a template for A (diagram 1). Cut fabric into five 3" strips. You will need 64 A pieces from dark prints.

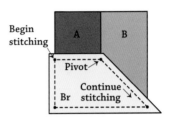

diagram 4

Make a template for B/Br (diagram 1). Cut fabric into eight 5¼" strips. Cut B/Br pieces as shown in diagram 2. You will need 64 B medium and 64 Br light pieces.

Arrange your pieces on a flat surface or a design wall to create a pleasing look.

diagram 5

Start sewing by stitching 1 A piece to the short side of 1 B piece. Stop ¼" from the corner and back stitch (diagram 3).

Next sew a BR to the A/B unit, stitching across A. Pivot the needle and continue sewing to the ¼" seam allowance (diagram 4).

Sew 3 more units the same way (diagram 5).

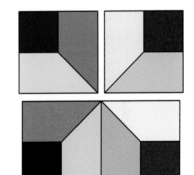

diagram 6

Sew 2 units together. Match the 2 sets in the center, with 2 seams going to the right and the bottom 2 seams to the left. Pin in the center and pin across the block.

Sew the 4 units together keeping the squares to the outside corners (diagram 6).

Measure the quilt top and cut 4 inner border pieces 1½" x 33½" (or your measurements) and sew onto the top and the bottom and the 2 sides.

Repeat to cut and sew 4 outer border pieces 3" x 39½" (or your measurements) onto the 2 sides, then the top and the bottom.

Press, baste, and quilt. Bind using your favorite method. Sew on a sleeve and a quilt label.

RIGHT: NELSON'S VICTORY, 38½" x 38½". Made by Peggy Weichel, Sorrento, Florida.

OCEAN WAVES

Made by Dee Danley-Brown
El Dorado Hills, California
(See page 83)

Dee used her hand-dyed gray fabric for the center squares and the light triangles.

Block Size	Sample Quilt	Twin	Queen
12" finished	36" x 36"	60" x 84"	84" x 96"
Fabric (yards)			
A (6½" x 6½")	½	1¼	6
B (Triangles)	2½	5	4
Backing	1¼	5½	8¾
Binding	Use leftover scraps	Use leftover scraps	Use leftover scraps
Construction			
Block arrangement	3 x 3	5 x 7	7 x 8
Total blocks	9	35	56

Read the Basic Directions (pages 6-11) before starting this project.

Make a template for A (diagram 1). Cut fabric into 9 strips 7" wide. Or use your 6½" square ruler and cut 9.

Make a template for B (diagram 1). Cut fabric into thirty-six 2½" strips. You will need 432 B pieces. Cut 216 from light scraps; cut 216 from dark scraps.

diagram 1

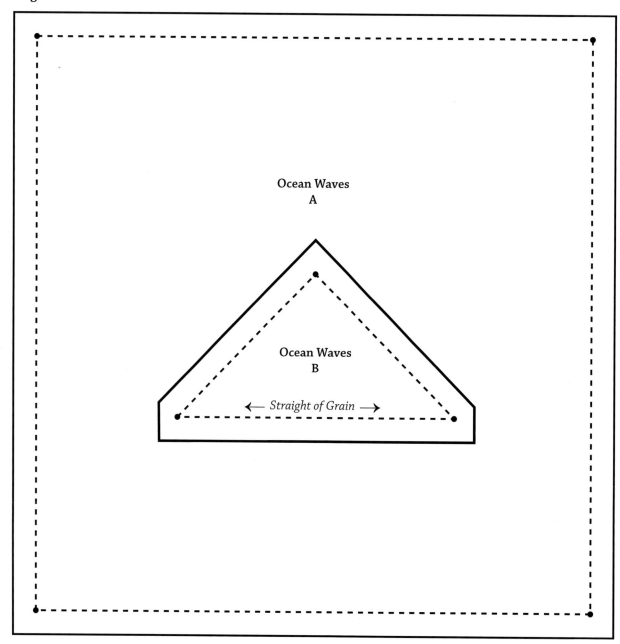

Ocean Waves
A

Ocean Waves
B

← *Straight of Grain* →

Arrange your pieces on a flat surface or a design wall to create a pleasing look.

Stitch pieces together in sections (diagram 2). Sew the seams end to end and backstitch.

See diagram 3 to assemble all of the sections into a 12½" block.

Sew 3 blocks together into 1 row making sure to match the points. Sew the 3 rows together.

Press, baste, and quilt.

Sew all of your leftover scraps together that are at least 2 inches wide to create the binding and use your favorite binding technique.

Sew on a sleeve and a quilt label.

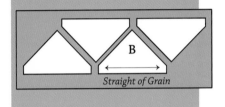

Tip:

○ When cutting the triangles (B), place the base or long side on the straight of the grain.

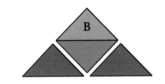

Straight of Grain

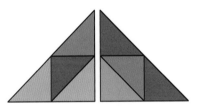

diagram 2

diagram 3

LEFT: OCEAN WAVES, 36" x 36". Made by Dee Danley-Brown, El Dorado Hills, California.

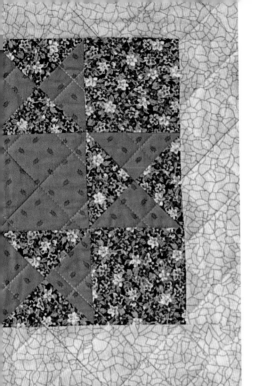

OHIO STAR

Made by Rosalba Kite, Kutztown, Pennsylvania
Machine quilted by Margrette Carr, San Diego, California
(See page 87)

Pay attention to colors when creating your blocks. Some have light centers and others have dark centers; note where the triangles are light or dark. Also, pay attention to contrast; see how different the top right and bottom left blocks in the sample quilt are relative to the other blocks. Both looks are valid, just different.

Block Size	Sample Quilt	Twin	Queen
9" finished	40" x 40"	63" x 90"	88" x 96"
Fabric (yards)			
A (3" Square finished) & B (Triangle)	1¼ (assorted scraps)	4½ (assorted scraps)	6 (assorted scraps)
Sashing	1	☆	☆
Border	¼	☆	☆
Flat piping (flange)	¼	☆	☆
Backing	1¼	5	8¾
Binding	¼	½	¾
Construction			
Block arrangement	3 x 3	7 x 10	11 x 12
Total blocks	9	70	132

☆ The choice is yours.

OHIO STAR

Read the Basic Directions (pages 6-11) before starting this project.

Make a template for A—a 3½" square. Cut fabric into five 4" strips. You will need 45 A pieces.

Make a template for B (diagram 1). Cut fabric into eight 2½" strips. You will need 144 B pieces.

diagram 1

Tips:

○ Lay the B template (triangle) on the fabric strip so the shapes nest to save fabric. Remember to move the template about ⅛" between cuts.

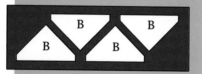

○ Measure your top before cutting long strips such as sashing and borders.

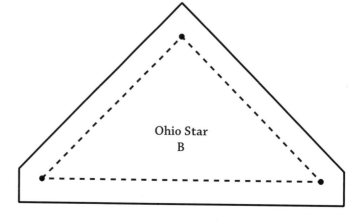

Arrange your pieces on a flat surface or a design wall to create a pleasing look. Place triangles of lights and darks opposite each other (diagram 2).

diagram 2

Sew a light and a dark triangle together along the straight edges and repeat (diagram 3).

Sew the triangles together along the diagonal edges alternating the dark and light pieces to make a square (diagram 4).

diagram 3

Make 3 more units. Then cut 5 A pieces. These 9 units will make 1 Ohio Star block.

To sew the block together, sew the top and bottom rows to the middle row. Be sure to match the seams carefully. Alternate the pressed direction of the seams with the top set going to the right and the bottom to the left (diagram 5).

diagram 4

Before the sashing is added, square up the blocks.

Cut 4 strips of sashing 2½" x 35". Cut 12 strips 2½" x 9½".

Sew the 12 strips to the top and bottom of each block. Use the 4 strips to join the top together.

diagram 5

For the border, cut 2 strips 1½" x 36½". Cut 2 strips 1½" x 35".

Sew the top and bottom borders on first. Sew on the 2 side borders.

To add the flange, see the BOW TIE instructions (pages 12–16).

Press, baste, and quilt. Use your favorite binding method. Sew on a sleeve and a quilt label.

RIGHT: OHIO STAR, 40" x 40". Made by Rosalba Kite, Kutztown, Pennsylvania. Machine quilted by Margrette Carr, San Diego, California.

GALLERY

RIGHT: OHIO STAR, 38" x 38". Made by Margrette Carr, San Diego, California.

LEFT: OHIO STAR, 36" x 36". Made by Rosalba Kite, Kutztown, Pennsylvania. Machine quilted by Margrette Carr, San Diego, California.

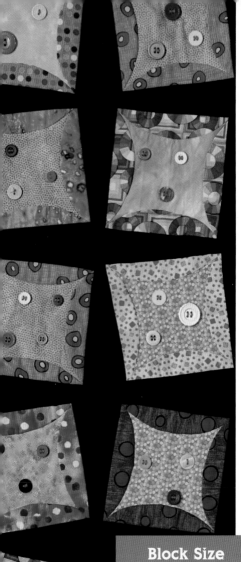

ROBBING PETER TO PAY PAUL

Made by Stevii Graves
Leesburg, Virginia
(See page 92)

This block is usually sewn side-to-side, but Stevii added black background strips around each block, then trimmed it at an angle, and added buttons for embellishment.

Block Size	Sample Quilt	Twin	Queen
5" finished	46" x 51"	65" x 90"	85" x 95"
Fabric (yards)			
A & B	3¼ (assorted scraps)	5 (assorted scraps)	7 (assorted scraps)
Border, background strips, and binding	2 (black)	☆	☆
Backing	3	5½	9½
Construction			
Block arrangement	7 x 8	13 x 18	17 x 19
Total blocks	56	234	323

☆ The choice is yours.

ROBBING PETER TO PAY PAUL

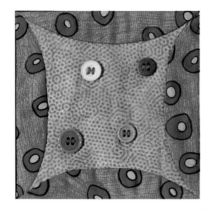

Read the Basic Directions (pages 6–11) before starting this project.

Make a template for A (diagram 1). Cut fabric into ten 6" strips. You will need 56 A pieces.

Make a template for B (diagram 1). Cut fabric into thirty-two 2" strips. You will need 224 B pieces.

Cut black border fabric into 2 pieces 45½" x 2½" and 2 pieces 47½" x 2½".

diagram 1

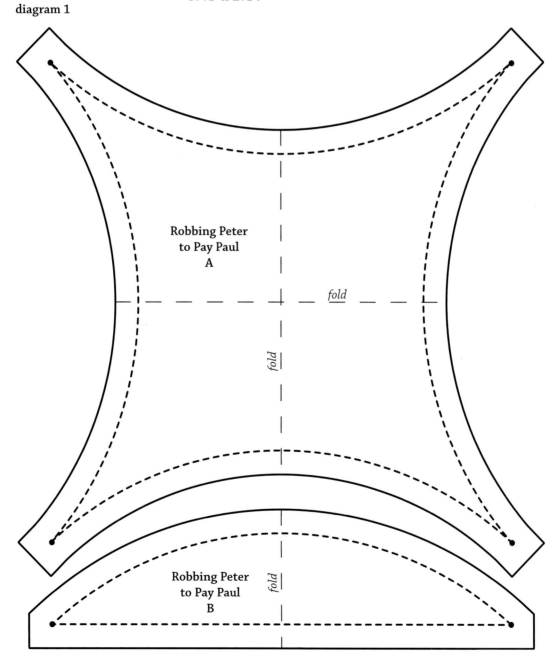

Robbing Peter
to Pay Paul
A

fold

fold

Robbing Peter
to Pay Paul
B

fold

Cut black background fabric into 112 pieces 2" x 5¼" and 112 pieces 2" x 8¼".

Set these all aside.

Fold A in half vertically and horizontally to find the center (diagram 1). Fold B in half to find the center (diagram 1).

Pin B to the top of A and pin across, easing in if necessary with pins (diagram 2). Sew B on opposite sides of A and finger press A toward the outside. Sew on the remaining sides in the same manner. The block should now measure 5½" (diagram 3). Sew 55 more blocks.

Tips:

○ You may want to wait until your top is pieced to measure it before cutting border strips. If so, set aside some fabric so you can cut the strips in long pieces.

○ Be sure there is at least ½" of surround fabric under the ruler before cutting. This will insure that there is some surround fabric on all sides of the block, plus a ¼" seam allowance.

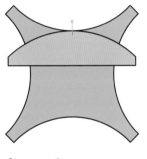

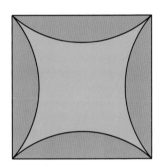

diagram 2   diagram 3

Stevii added a bit of creativity to her "Paul" and sewed 2" strips to each side of the block (diagram 4). Place a 6½" ruler on the surrounded block (diagram 5.) Tilt the ruler to the right and trim (diagram 6).

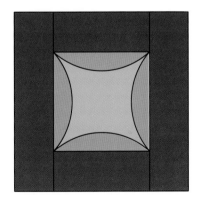

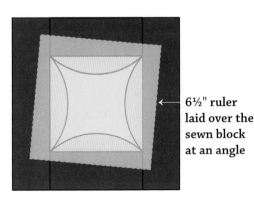

6½" ruler laid over the sewn block at an angle

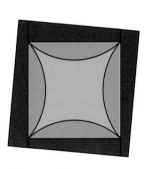

diagram 6

diagram 4   diagram 5

Robbing Peter to Pay Paul

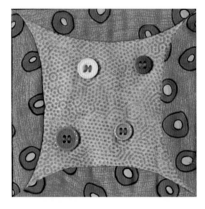

On the next surround block, tilt the ruler to the left before cutting and follow same as above.

Sew the blocks together 7 across and 8 rows down, carefully matching the seam allowances.

Sew the borders to the 2 sides, then to the top and bottom.

Press, baste, and quilt. Use your favorite binding method. Sew on a sleeve and add a quilt label.

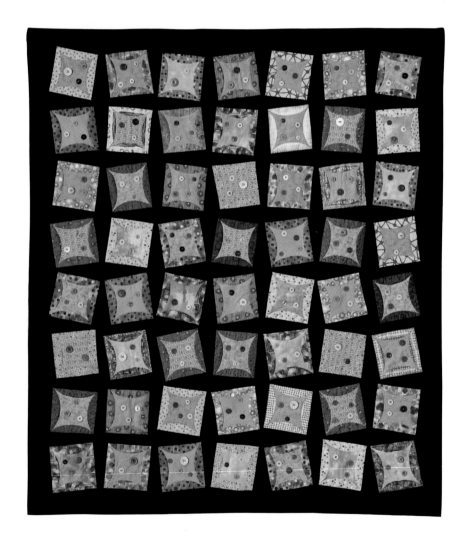

LEFT: Robbing Peter to Pay Paul, 46" x 51". Made by Stevii Graves, Leesburg, Virginia.

GALLERY

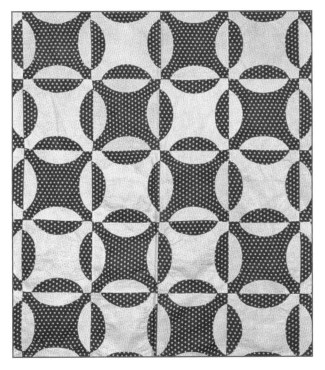

ABOVE: ROBBING PETER TO PAY PAUL, detail. Antique quilt top in the collection of the author.

BELOW: ROBBING PETER TO PAY PAUL, 34" x 39". Made by Stevii Graves & Dorothy Thompson, McLean, Virginia.

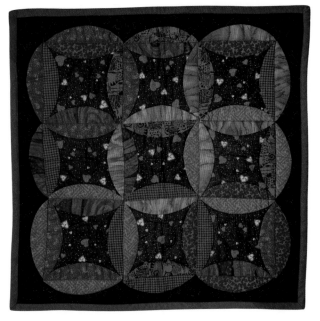

ABOVE: ROBBING PETER TO PAY PAUL, 18" x 18". Made by Kimberley Graf, San Diego, California.

BELOW: ROBBING PETER TO PAY PAUL, 19½" x 29". Made by the author.

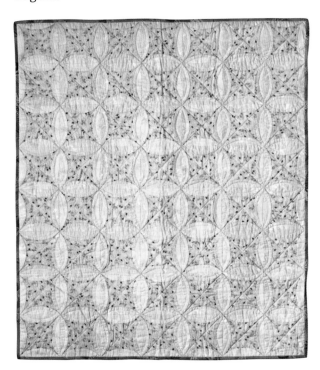

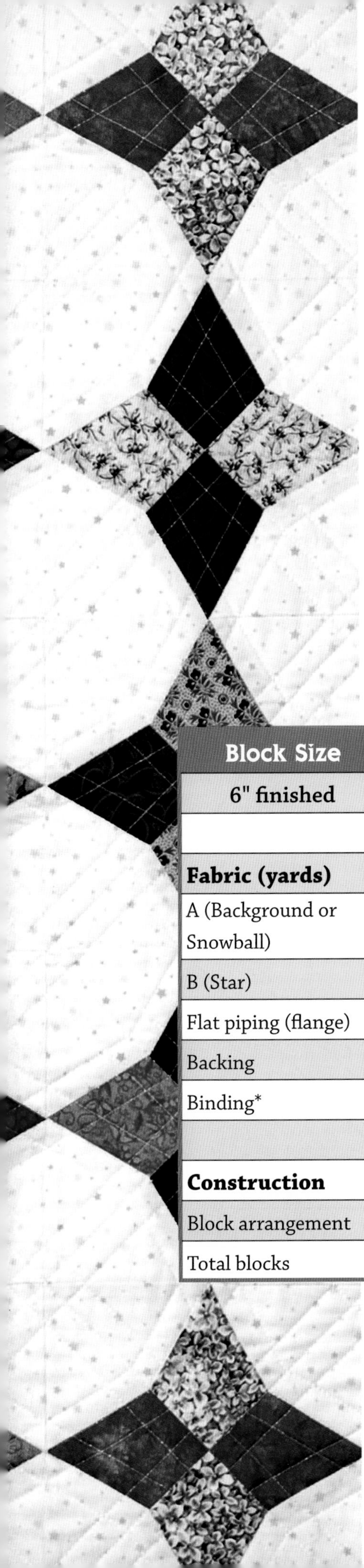

SNOWBALL

Made by Margrette Carr
San Diego, California
(See page 98)

Margrette used pastel star fabric for the Snowballs (background) to enhance the stars in her quilt.

Block Size	Sample Quilt	Twin	Queen
6" finished	36" x 42"	66" x 90"	84" x 96"
Fabric (yards)			
A (Background or Snowball)	1	2	2½
B (Star)	½	1½	2
Flat piping (flange)	¼ (9" x 36")		
Backing	1¼	5	8¾
Binding*	¼	½	¾
Construction			
Block arrangement	6 x 7	11 x 15	14 x 16
Total blocks	42	165	224

* Straight grain.

Read the Basic Directions (pages 6–11) before starting this project.

Make a template for A (diagram 1). Cut fabric into fourteen 4" strips. You will need 168 A pieces.

Make a template for B (diagram 1). Cut fabric into thirteen 4" strips. You will need 168 B pieces.

Arrange your pieces on a flat surface or a design wall to create a pleasing look.

Begin by laying A (the Snowball) on the straight grain of the fabric, keeping a 90-degree angle so the other 2 sides are on the bias (diagram 2).

diagram 1

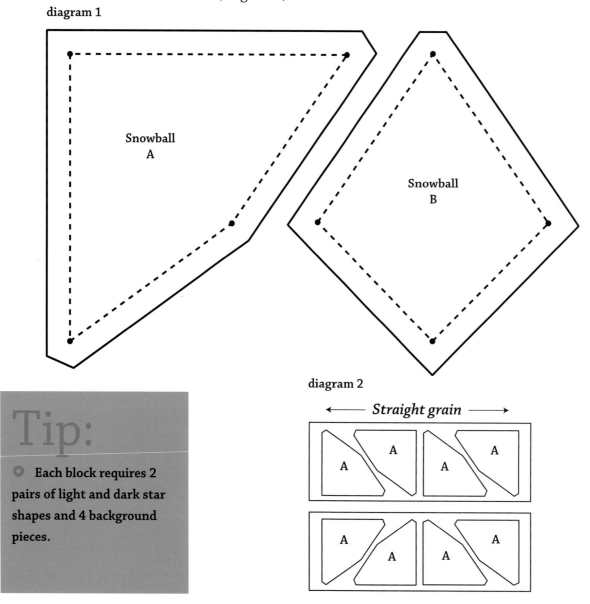

Snowball
A

Snowball
B

diagram 2

Straight grain

Tip:

○ **Each block requires 2 pairs of light and dark star shapes and 4 background pieces.**

Sew 2 B pieces together and finger press (diagram 3).

Next, match the centers and pin. Pin across, starting and stopping ¼" from the edge (diagram 4).

Begin sewing the background piece, starting at the straight edge. Stop ¼" before the star seam, drop the needle, and rotate the background. Holding the background in your finger or with a stiletto, continue to sew the background pieces to the star side (diagram 5).

Repeat to add 3 more backgrounds to the block.

Sew the remaining star pairs and background pieces to make 41 more blocks.

Sew the blocks together to make rows, then sew the rows together, being careful to match the seams (diagram 6).

Press, baste, and quilt.

For the flat piping, cut 1" wide fabric, press it in half lengthwise wrong sides together, and sew it along the edge of the quilt top with a ⅛" seam before adding the binding.

Use your favorite binding method. Sew on a sleeve and a quilt label.

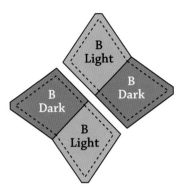

diagram 3

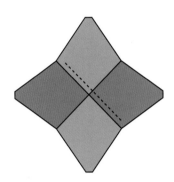

diagram 4

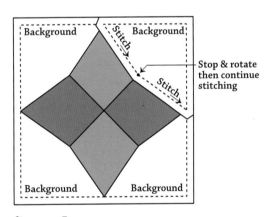

diagram 5

diagram 6

SNOWBALL

GALLERY

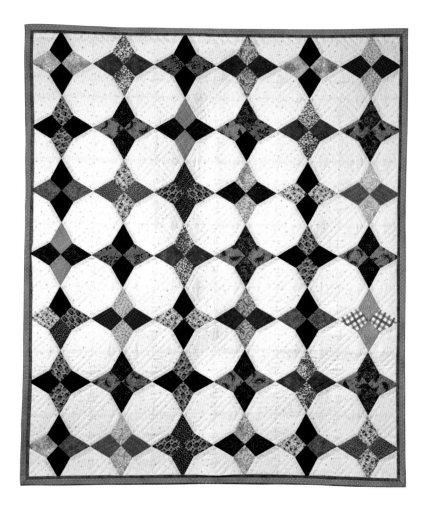

RIGHT: SNOWBALL, 36" x 42".
Made by Margrette Carr, San
Diego, California.

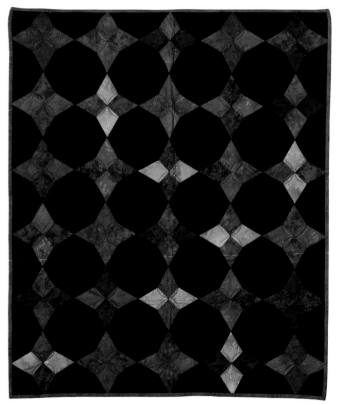

LEFT: SNOWBALL, 30" x 35". Made
by the author.

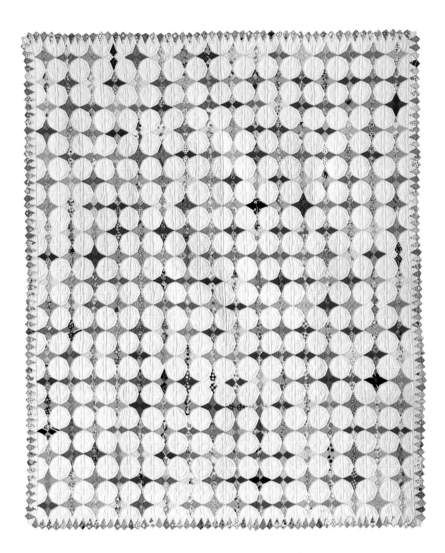

LEFT: SNOWBALL, 70" x 84". Antique quilt in the collection of the author. Hand quilted by Laura Lipski, Lindenhurst, New York.

RIGHT: SNOWBALL, 22" x 22". Made by the author.

SPINNING SPOOLS

Made by Diane Weber
San Jose, California
(See page 103)

This quilt can be made of scraps, homespun, Christmas prints, etc. It has so many looks depending on the fabric choice. Feel free to let your creativity explore!

Block Size	Sample Quilt	Twin	Queen
8" finished	40" x 40"	64" x 88"	88" x 96"
Fabric (yards)			
A & B*	3¼ (assorted scraps)	4¾	7
Backing	1¼	5	8½
Binding	¼	½	1
Construction			
Block arrangement	5 x 5	8 x 11	11 x 12
Total blocks	25	88	132

* To make the binding from one of the B fabrics as shown in the sample quilt, add ¼ yard of that particular fabric to the assorted scraps total. If you do that, you do not need additional binding fabric.

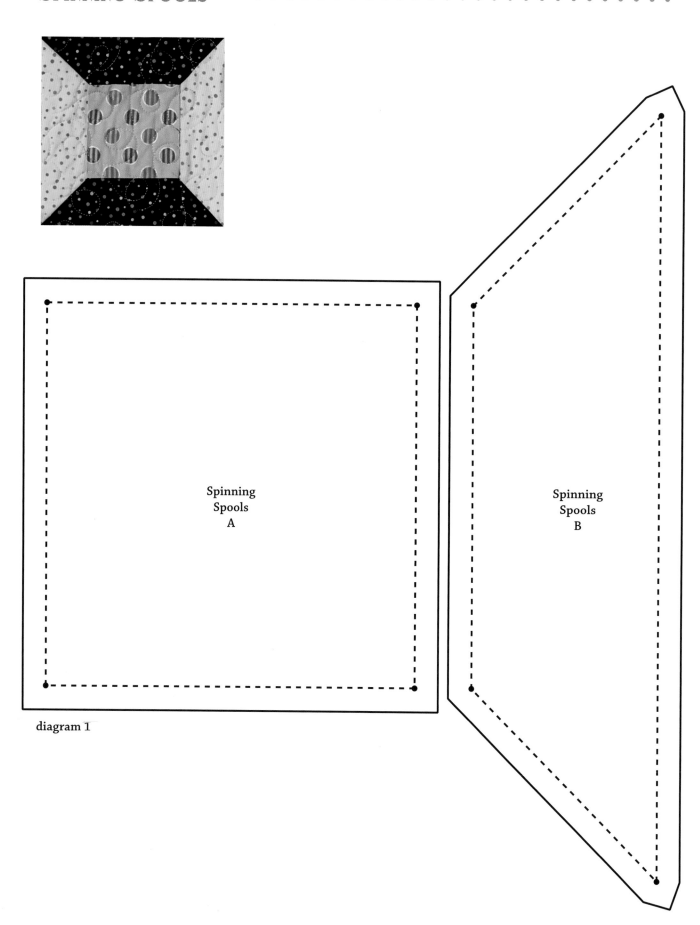

Spinning
Spools
A

Spinning
Spools
B

diagram 1

Read the Basic Directions (pages 6–11) before starting this project.

The A template is a 4½" square (diagram 1). Make 1. Cut fabric into four 5" strips or use 5" charm squares for the center square. You will need 25 A pieces.

Make a B template (diagram 1). Cut fabric into twenty-seven 3" strips. Rotate the template down the strips to save fabric (diagram 2). You will need 50 light B and 50 dark B pieces.

Arrange the pieces on a flat surface or a design wall to create a pleasing look.

Sew a B piece to opposite sides of the A square, starting and stopping ¼" from the ends; use a backstitch each time. If you start with 2 lights, the other sides will be 2 darks.

Next, pin one side of a B piece to the adjacent B piece. Stitch from the outside in towards the center square (diagram 3, seam 1). Pin match the B piece to the A square and stitch from ¼" to ¼" (seam 2). Pin and sew the last seam to the outside of the block (seam 3). Repeat the same steps for the other side of the block.

Make 24 more blocks in the same manner.

Join the blocks into rows, paying attention to alternate the direction of the spools as in the sample quilt photograph. Sew the rows together, matching the seam allowances.

Press, baste, and quilt. Use your favorite binding method. Sew on a sleeve and a quilt label.

Tips:

○ Turn the blocks so you have vertical and horizontal spools.

○ Start and stop ¼" from the edge when sewing these units together. If you have a ¼" foot on your machine, it will make this a breeze. If not, mark your ¼" seam allowances, then mark a dot at each corner.

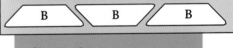

diagram 2

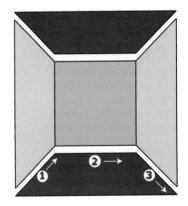

diagram 3

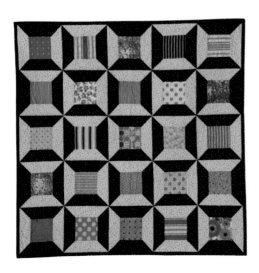

LEFT: SPINNING SPOOLS, 40" x 40". Made by Diane Weber, San Jose, California.

TIPSY-TURVY

Made by Linda Gresham
Laredo, Texas
(See page 108)

This is a wonderful scrap quilt. As a suggestion, you can turn the blocks a quarter turn to give it a whimsical look.

Block Size	Sample Quilt	Twin	Queen
4" finished	27½" x 35½"	64" x 88"	84" x 92"
Fabric (yards)			
A & B	1	5¼	7
Border	1 (2½" x 36")	☆	☆
Backing	1	5	4¾
Binding	¼	½	¾
Construction			
Block arrangement	6 x 8	16 x 22	21 x 23
Total blocks	48	352	483

☆   The choice is yours.

Read the Basic Directions (pages 6–11) before starting this project.

Make a template for A (diagram 1). Cut fabric into five 2" strips. You will need 96 A pieces.

Make a B template (diagram 1). Cut fabric into ten 3" strips. You will need 96 B pieces.

Arrange your pieces on a flat surface or a design wall to create a pleasing look.

Begin by stitching 2 B pieces together, starting and stopping at the ¼" seam allowance (diagram 2).

Tips:

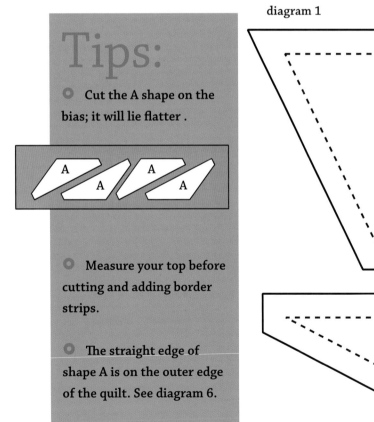

○ Cut the A shape on the bias; it will lie flatter .

○ Measure your top before cutting and adding border strips.

○ The straight edge of shape A is on the outer edge of the quilt. See diagram 6.

diagram 1

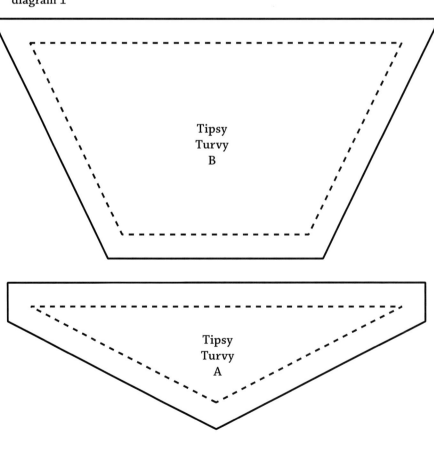

Tipsy
Turvy
B

Tipsy
Turvy
A

Pin, pin, pin, inserting A pieces into B (diagram 3). Sew seams 1–4. Finger press A toward B. Make 95 more blocks (diagram 4).

There are 6 blocks across and 8 rows down in the sample quilt. Pin the blocks together to make a row, and sew the rows together (diagram 5). Be careful not to stretch the fabric.

To make the border, cut 2 strips 2½" x 28½" for the top and bottom. Cut 2 strips 2½" x 31¾" for the sides.

Linda added a little zest to her quilt by using leftover A pieces and appliquéing them to the border. Using the starch method, make a template with heat-resistant material.

Dip a small paintbrush into liquid starch and paint it on the reverse side of the fabric.

Using a hot dry iron, press the ¼" turn under allowance onto the template. Arrange the prepared A pieces around the border of the quilt. Pin in place.

Use matching thread to appliqué the pieces in place being careful not to stretch them.

Baste, quilt, and bind using your favorite method. The sample quilt binding was cut on the bias; with the striped fabric, it adds interest to the quilt. Make a quilt label and sew on a sleeve.

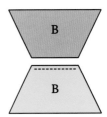

diagram 2

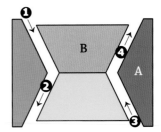

diagram 3

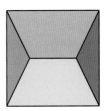

diagram 4

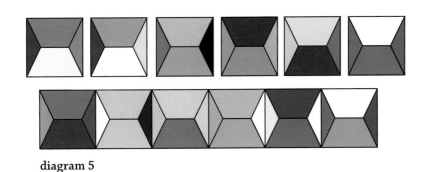

diagram 5

raw edge

diagram 6

RIGHT: TIPSY TURVY, 34½" x 35½".
Made by Linda Gresham, Laredo,
Texas.

LEFT: TIPSY TURVY II, 27½" x
35½". Made by Linda Gresham,
Laredo, Texas.

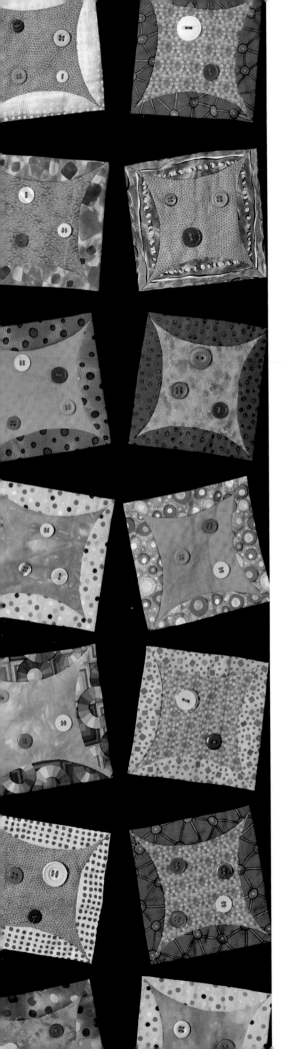

RESOURCES

Templates

Come Quilt With Me
3903 Ave I
Brooklyn, NY 11210
www.comequiltwithme.com

Add-a-Quarter™ Ruler

CM Designs, Inc.
7968 Kelty Trail
Franktown, CO 80116
www.addaquarter.com

Rotary Mats and Cutters, Template Plastic

Prym Consumer USA, Inc.
PO Box 5028
Spartanburg, SC 29304
www.prym-consumer-usa.com

LEFT: ROBBING PETER TO PAY PAUL, detail. Full quilt on page 92.

ABOUT THE AUTHOR

Pat Yamin, president and founder of Come Quilt With Me, is well known in the quilting industry. She has appeared on many television and radio quilt shows, the most recent being *The Quilt Show* with Ricky Tims and Alex Anderson. Her company manufactures templates and other tools that assure accuracy and shorten the time necessary to make a quilt.

Often asked to exhibit her antique quilt collection at major quilt shows all over America, Pat's fondness for old textiles and patterns is the driving force behind her creativity. She truly believes that what is old is new again, and knows that if acrylic templates, cutting mats, and rotary cutters had been available to our quilting ancestors, they would have used them!

For more than 40 years Pat has been designing quilt patterns and templates, making quilts, teaching quilting, judging, leading seminars, and writing quilt books. *Two-Patch Scrap Quilts* is her fourth quilting book. The others are *One-Patch Scrap Quilts* (AQS, 2007), *Back to Basics: Quilt Templates and Patterns Explained* (AQS, 2003), and *Look What I See Quilts* (American School of Needlework, 2001).

In addition to designing, teaching, traveling, and vending at quilt shows, Pat organizes and runs an annual quilting retreat in Michigan each August.

In 2011 as Come Quilt With Me celebrates its 30th anniversary, Pat strongly feels that a huge part of her success is due to her loyal customers.

If you are interested in learning more about Pat Yamin and Come Quilt With Me, visit her website, www.comequiltwithme.com.

LEFT AND OPPOSITE: HUMMINGBIRD, detail. Antique quilt top in author's collection.

MORE AQS BOOKS · · · · · · · · · · · ·

This is only a small selection of the books available from the American Quilter's Society. AQS books are known worldwide for timely topics, clear writing, beautiful color photos, and accurate illustrations and patterns. The following books are available from your local bookseller, quilt shop, or public library.

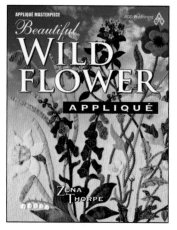

#8526

#8146

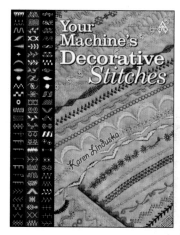

#8353

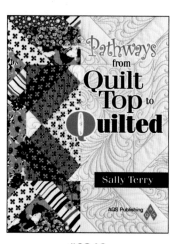

#8348

#8349

#8355

#8351

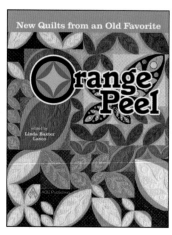

#8350

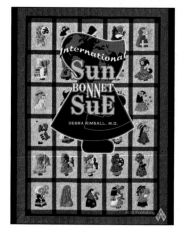

#8347